Personnel
and Profit

Hugo Fair is Development Director of Percom. After qualifying as an accountant, he joined Burroughs Machines (now Unisys) as a graduate trainee and helped develop the first computer systems at the Stock Exchange. He managed a European project for American Express aimed at decentralising financial management to individual country operations and then worked in sales and marketing for SIA, the UK division of France's largest computer services firm. He subsequently helped found a group of companies providing HR services to the high-technology sector. He has contributed papers to several books and is an Associate Member of the IPM.

Personnel and Profit:

the pay-off from people

Hugo Fair

Institute of Personnel Management

First published in 1992

Phototypeset by The Comp-Room, Aylesbury
and printed in Great Britain by
Short Run Press, Exeter

British Library Cataloguing in Publication Data

Fair, Hugo
  Personnel and Profit: Pay-off from People
  I. Title
  658.3

  ISBN 0-85292-462-3

Contents

Acknowledgements

I am extremely grateful to the Institute of Personnel Management for providing this platform which I hope readers will draw on for practical exercises that further integrate personnel into the mainstream of organisational strategy. Although a distillation of experiences gained over the last 17 years in accountancy, personnel and marketing, this book owes its existence to the encouragement of John Angel, Managing Director of Percom, as well as the unflagging support of my wife, Vivien. The understanding of past and present colleagues has been most helpful and I should particularly like to thank Carl Taylor ACA and Alastair Evans FIPM, for their assistance in validating financial terminology and personnel practices, respectively. Finally, my thanks go to Pete Holley, who produced graphs and illustrations of the highest quality at very short notice. All the opinions expressed or comments made are entirely my responsibility and do not necessarily reflect the views of either Percom or the IPM.

Introduction

'Well, what do they expect if they won't spend any money on . . . ?'
Such sentiments are expressed every day throughout the land by you,
me and most of our colleagues. And we're often not that selective as
to the choice of topic. Our frustration may be quite genuine, but the
inference – that some nameless group of people is obstructing us –
should be treated very sceptically.

The key point is that most decisions have one or more cost factors
associated with them. Either additional costs are incurred or existing
resources are redirected. In most cases, of course, we all know that
this is worthwhile because it will lead to our planned objectives –
reducing costs and improving productivity. You can't get more out of
your people unless they are properly trained and rewarded, any more
than you can reduce costs if all your time is spent controlling either
unauthorised absenteeism or a staff turnover rate that is listed in *The
Guinness Book of Records*! So why do I say that we are misleading
ourselves if we blame any lack of investment on others?

Well, firstly, we often seem unwilling to be very specific in identifying who the obstructors are. It is much easier to blame a totally
anonymous 'them' or an impersonal group, such as the Board or the
Finance department. And, secondly, we make no effort to explain
the request for any investment in terms that the other party
appreciates or can comprehend.

In fact, Personnel has often managed to acquire a particularly
unenviable reputation as the least numerate function in the organisation. When there is often apparent disagreement even on the true
headcount, it can be difficult for others readily to trust your grasp of
figures. Whilst this is seen as a slur by most of us, it is not entirely an
unwarranted one.

It is quite natural for people to be at least wary, if not downright
suspicious, of things they don't understand. It is, unfortunately, also
natural for people to base their judgements on what they have personally experienced. So, if you approach your Finance Director with
a request for an increased training budget, think first. Can he or she
automatically be expected to understand the benefits of the investment? Have you expressed these benefiits in terms that they are used
to? If not, what are the chances that at some time in their life they
have been on an expensive course that they didn't enjoy and there-

1

fore believe was a waste of time and money? How do you rate your chances of success – and do you think your credibility has been improved?

Now try putting yourself in the role of the Financial Director. Is there any evidence that previous investments in similar training generated the benefits that were promised? Were these quantifiable, anyway? In what way might the current request be a better investment than myriad competing claims – including others from Personnel?

So what am I suggesting you do about all this? It's hard enough keeping up with legislation, new fashions and terminology in HR and the impact of changing technology, not to mention the usual firefighting and support needs of other departments. I appear to be encouraging you also to become an accountant and a marketeer, with possibly a dash of statistician and even computer guru, so you can quantify the costs and benefits of personnel proposals and gain support for them.

Well, not really. You don't have to become any of these, but you do have to have a reasonable idea of their worlds and their perceptions of how they each contribute to your organisation. In particular, you need to be able to interpret their seemingly secret languages and give them the confidence that they can rely on your understanding of their needs.

The good news is that this doesn't mean that you have to learn several new languages. There is, broadly speaking, one common numerical framework that can be made to represent any organisation in which we operate. Whether private, public, entrepreneurial or charitable, they all have to operate within financial limits imposed, largely, through their own performance.

This book is intended to give you the background to some of that general framework and, in particular, to help you identify and quantify those areas in which you can most profitably make your mark – both personally and for your organisation. Each may use slightly different performance measurements, but they will usually be applied consistently.

Once you have grasped what the measures are for your organisation, you need to place any personnel proposals within the right framework so as to ensure they are correctly interpreted by your colleagues. You may find that you better understand their problems and you are certainly in a better position to be seen as part of any strategic decision-making processes.

Finally, a warning. This book makes no attempt to resolve any of the rather academic issues that often seem to split our profession or to give guidance on best HR practices. It also cannot claim to provide a magic key that will instantly solve one or more of your current problems. It is very much a book to be applied by you, the reader, to your own organisation as a practical support tool. As such, it can be re-used time and again to look at different aspects of your business or to check the effectiveness of earlier decisions. The opportunity for Personnel to play the same game, with the same rules, as all the other functions is now there. Please help yourself.

PART ONE:
THE BUSINESS OF PEOPLE

In the last two or three years it has become almost impossible to pick up an annual report or to read a general management magazine without finding a phrase like 'Our people are our business.' When you look beneath the surface, however, doubts soon emerge about the real level of commitment to this idea. As the most basic guide, it can be instructive to see how many organisations have a Personnel Director on the Board, or can demonstrate a strong HR content in their corporate strategies.

It is unlikely that the boardrooms of Britain are solely occupied by the mendacious or incompetent, so why does this gap still persist between their espoused beliefs and the evidence of their actions? One problem is the use of a single language for Finance and Personnel without understanding that the same word may have very different connotations.

What, for example, about the claims of Managing Directors that 'Our people are our greatest asset', particularly in the service sector (where staff are generally the 'product' being sold and therefore the assets employed to generate revenue)? Whilst the colloquial definition of an 'asset' may simply be a resource that generates benefits, this is not totally equivalent to the financial meaning of an item that has a value on the balance sheet. Plant machinery may well be both of these simultaneously, but people are not such a simple matter. One City analyst is reported to have contemptuously pointed out that you can hardly have balance-sheet assets that get in the lift, go home every night and may never return. This is not to say that employees do not have a quantifiable value (and cost) to their organisation, but it is necessary first to understand how organisations themselves are often measured and valued – by themselves and by others.

Chapter 1

Finance – Organisational Effectiveness

The senior decision-making forum in any organisation, usually a Board of Directors, has many formal and some legal responsibilities. However, it is probably true to say that in essence they have one overriding responsibility: to ensure the continuing operation of the organisation. As a direct consequence, they will seek to set and achieve a variety of financial targets which usually include profits – whether to return to shareholders or to re-invest in growing the organisation.

In most cases, they will have also had the foresight to identify in advance some quantifiable measurements of organisational effectiveness, so that progress towards the financial targets can be monitored. Companies which fail (or have to be rescued) usually turn out to have inadequate financial measures of controls. Most of these are expressed in purely financial terms, such as earnings per share, asset turnover, profit-before-tax, liquidity and other basic measures. However, some include a strong 'employee cost' factor which it would be useful for a personnel professional to appreciate.

Some of these measurements are designed for operational use within the organisation and some are calculated by outside bodies. The most important fact, however, is that nearly all are expressed as a single value (often a ratio); it is *changes* in this figure that are seen as the primary indicator of organisational health and efficiency. As with all aspects of quality, the objective should be continuous, usually small, improvements – not a magical target that can be achieved and then forgotten.

Operational Measurements

The first thing you must do is to define the items that you will use to calculate your measurements, in order to ensure they are consistent over the period for which you are monitoring changes. For the sake of simplicity I have assumed the following definitions at all times, although you may choose your own:

7

Full-time equivalent (FTE) is defined as all staff (including part-time and contract) that worked for more than 15 hours per week in that month.

Headcount (HC) is defined as the total FTE at month-end.

Revenues (RE) are defined as total operating income (i.e. total sales) for the period stated.

Expenses (EX) are defined as all operating expenditure excluding tax, interest and extraordinary items.

Profit (PR) is defined as operating revenues (RE) less expenses (EX).

Compensation (CO) includes all staff cash rewards or incentives, such as salary, wages, overtime, bonuses, commissions – including employee-related taxation (PAYE, NI, etc).

Benefits (BE) includes all other forms of individual remuneration (whether or not currently taxed as a 'benefit in kind'), such as cars, pensions and loans.

Without claiming to be a truly exhaustive list, it is very likely that at least one of the following is used as a key indicator by your organisation. Subtle variations may be in use, so you should attempt to discover the exact definitions which are applied. Nevertheless, they should always provide you with useful insights.

Sales per Employee (SPE)

This is probably the most basic and common measurement of general employee productivity. It can be calculated monthly, quarterly or on a cumulative year-to-date (YTD) basis and monitored accordingly. The formula is as simple as dividing revenues by the average number of employees for that period:

$$SPE = \frac{RE}{HC}.$$

The attraction of the SPE ratio is that it is easy and quick to calculate – with an increase in SPE being desirable. It, therefore, provides an almost instant indication of any changing trend in fortunes (good or bad), once you have enough historical data to understand the level of variation that your own organisation should expect in the normal course of events.

As a brief exercise, you may like to calculate the SPE for your own organisation at the year-end 1, 2, 3 and 4 years ago, and then also for the last 4 quarters. The trend (and rate of change) will, for instance, show up any period when you increased headcount to gear up for expansion – and the results if the growth in business did not transpire. Now try monitoring SPE every week or month, as appropriate, and see if it helps you to identify relevant headcount strategies more quickly and accurately.

The graph (Figure 1) shows a case where SPE decreased in both 1989 and 1991, although for very different reasons. The trend in 1989 was the result of a deliberate policy, based on a decision to invest in additional headcount so that advantage could be taken of the available revenue opportunities apparent in the previous year. Although it was expected that the headcount would increase faster than revenues initially, it was found that the slide in SPE could only be halted by curtailing the recruitment drive and waiting for a noticeable upturn in revenues.

Throughout 1990, revenue remained fairly static and headcount was allowed to do the same. As a result, rapidly falling revenues in 1991 have continued to run ahead of all attempts to reduce headcount

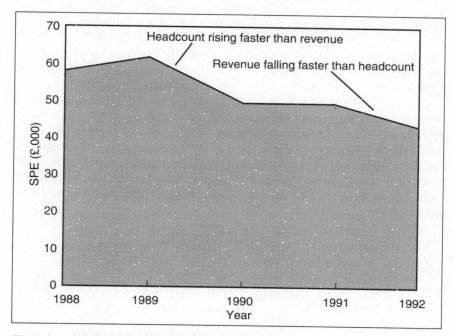

Figure 1   Changes in SPE over Time

through natural wastage and the organisation is faced with tough choices. Even if SPE had been monitored all the time there is no guarantee that the wrong decisions would not have been made, but at least the results of those decisions might have been apparent at a much earlier stage (i.e. the middle of 1990) and corrective action being simpler to implement.

Recovery Rate (RR)

This introduces a profitability element by comparing the costs of employees with the revenues delivered. The frequency of measurement varies but should be consistent within an organisation. The calculation is performed by consolidating compensation and benefits and then dividing the result by revenues:

$$RR = \frac{CO + BE}{RE}.$$

RR provides a quick indication of whether your organisation is obtaining more or less return on each pound it is investing directly in its people – with a decrease in RR being desirable. Whilst the effect of different influences (wastage, a new factory, etc) can be difficult to disentangle, the impact of additional investment should show through in improved RR later. As an example, you can try calculating the figures over a given period *both with and without the inclusion of a specific indirect employee cost* such as training.

The graph (Figure 2) shows that training was negligible in 1988 and 1989, when RR started to worsen. However, in 1990 there was considerable investment in training, and a slight improvement in RR, which became dramatic during 1991 (even when training was reduced during the year). Unless other factors contributed to a rise in revenues, this clearly shows the benefits of a training commitment successfully delivered. It also strongly implies the dangers of cutting back now.

Utilisation Rate (UR)

Some people prefer to reverse the calculation for RR, referring to it as the Utilisation Rate:

$$UR = \frac{RE}{CO + BE}.$$

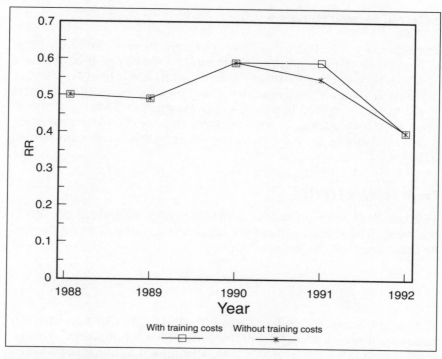

Figure 2   Changes in RR over Time

This provides a basic productivity measure, where an increase in UR is desirable. Whether you choose UR or RR, so long as you stick to one, measuring the change will be just as effective.

UR is probably easiest to understand when applied to a company whose prime business is re-selling the time of its employees (e.g. consultancies), but can be just as easily applied elsewhere. If RE is replaced with the major measurable output appropriate to your business (e.g. pints of milk delivered by a dairy or dustbins emptied by a refuse collection service), then you can obtain a figure for the UR.

Whatever the output used to give a value to RE, there is one golden rule. The calculation of UR must include the employee costs of the complete business unit, not just the cost of those employees directly delivering the RE. Failure to do this often results in support departments alternating between expansion and shrinkage without regard to any impact on the delivery of RE – and often totally out of phase with the requirements.

External Measurements

The efficiency, or otherwise, of your organisation is also likely to be of interest to outside parties. Their interest may appear benevolent or resemble a circling vulture; the only difference is likely to be your perception of their motives. However, in most cases they are less likely to be interested in gradual improvements within your operation. What they want to know is the performance of your organisation relative to others in the sector – in other words, your competitive strength.

Profit per Head (PH)

This is usually referred to, more correctly, as profit-before-tax (PBT) per head. The calculation is very simple, consisting of profit divided by the number of employees:

$$PH = \frac{PR}{HC}.$$

This amounts to a simplification of ROCE, an accountant's measure of return on capital employed, which is not solely based on employee-related costs or returns. Although it is not a particularly useful operational tool, there is a good reason for showing it. This is because, as mentioned earlier, some financial indicators are used as much, if not more, by outside parties – including competitors and other market predators. To these groups your PH rating, when compared to others in the market, may indicate that your organisation has a profit potential that is far from being achieved. If this is so and you are a private-sector company, your independence is threatened; if in the public sector, your funding may be reduced. It is almost certainly worthwhile, therefore, to calculate the PH rating of the major players and nearest relevant competitors in your market sector so you can identify your changing position in the league table. For instance, the table (Figure 3) shows that the Widget Co. is still in the leading 3 companies, although its PH has slipped significantly last year in comparison to some of its nearest competitors. You can also see how the dominant player managed to increase its PH in difficult trading conditions (and could be considering a bid for IBN). Crudco, an erstwhile competitor from 1989 who is now propping up the foot of the table, miscalculated badly last year and may not be around soon.

		1991 £	1990 £
1	Sunrise Industries	63,291	60,071
2	Widget Co	31,695	38,633
3	Nick Simon Software	27,688	20,749
4	Phoenix Enterprises	19,821	20,292
5	CSD plc	17,989	21,844
6	LoPanel	17,132	15,235
7	IBN	16,894	41,987
8	Virtual Systems	16,245	20,345
9	Cyclotron	14,834	20,942
10	Firefighter Research	12,872	(1,345)
88	Blue Box plc	(1,734)	(778)
89	Harcourt Res Assoc	(1,892)	108
90	Punter Inc	(2,038)	(898)
91	Crudco	(6,524)	18,323

Figure 3   Comparative PH Figures for Competing Companies

Compensation per Profit (CP)

This is virtually the same as PH, except that profit is being measured against the cost of employees rather than merely the number of them. The calculation, compared to PH, is also generally reversed:

$$CP = \frac{CO + BE}{PR}.$$

This has a potentially confusing effect in that the scale of CP ratios is not contiguous; if you sometimes move into losses (i.e. negative PR), then CP will become negative. So, although the 'best' CP is a small positive number (as close to zero as possible), the 'worst' is a small negative number. The range of possible values is represented on the graph (Figure 4).

As a result, a comparative chart of competitors might look like the example shown in Figure 5. The first five companies are making respectable profits, the next two are making minimal profits and the 8th and 9th small losses. Sunset Enterprises looks likely to be about to live up to its name.

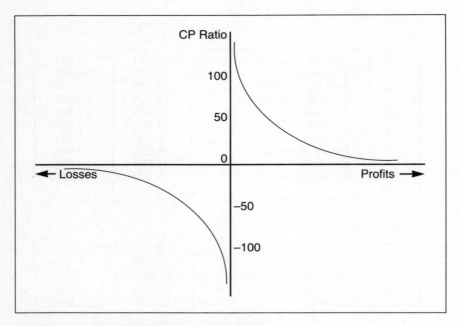

Figure 4   Possible Values for CP Ratios

A good deal of caution, however, is appropriate when using the CP ratio. Unless there is a very close connection between profits and compensation (i.e. most of the company receives the majority of pay as sales-only commission or as a profit-related bonus), it will fluctuate with any swings in profits. If the measurement is made frequently in an organisation where profits and losses alternate, CP will change from positive values to negative and back again, making interpretation hard. As a result, it is not very useful operationally but may indicate to a predator that a change in management could achieve an improvement in cost-effectiveness or controls. So you may be interested for that reason alone.

There are, as I have said, other measures and an almost infinite number of variations that can be applied. However, the point has hopefully been made that some major indicators of the financial performance and health of organisations *include personnel data*. They are used not just by accountants, but by financial planners, including specialists in acquisitions and mergers – within and outside your organisation.

Since much of the data is supplied by you in the first place and the

		1991
1	Baldric Enterprises	0.6
2	Porky Productions	1.1
3	Trifle plc	1.8
4	Plumb Networking	4.8
5	Nick Simon Systems	12.1
6	Softwhere Co	40.8
7	Fair Trading Inc	211.3
8	Muldoon Systems	−748.6
9	Dorn Risers	−198.5
10	Sunset Enterprises	−72.1

Figure 5 Comparative CP Figures

rest is fairly accessible, you can quickly create a set of historic data and then carry out comparisons on a regular basis. You can rest assured that, whether you do or not, *others* will – and they may not have the best interests of you or your organisation at heart.

Chapter 2

Personnel – an Influential Strategy

It is unlikely to come as any surprise to you that the financial implications of human resource decisions are infrequently understood and are, at best, monitored in most organisations at a macro level. The cumulative effect may well be measured, but little attempt will be made to separate out other contributory factors or to identify the impact of individual strategies, let alone each decision.

More and more organisations have identified the importance of employee costs as a contributory factor to the health of their business, but few have moved beyond a determination that they must therefore be carefully controlled. The problem is that nothing can really be controlled in a vacuum; you have to identify a target, after taking into account the effect on other aspects of the business, and then plan how to achieve it. Otherwise, controlling costs becomes merely a euphemism for reducing them – usually without understanding the knock-on effects.

If it is uncomfortable not being allowed to make important decisions, it is surely more so to be measured inaccurately and against unknown targets. So, as well as improving your knowledge of how others may be measuring your organisation, it is worth applying similar calculations to areas of the business that are more directly under your control. You may be surprised to find out how much impact some of your decisions can have on the key financial indicators. And these insights should help you to educate others into making more informed assessments of your own and your department's performance.

Defensive Measurements

These are ratios that are, in themselves, of no strategic value but can be helpful in putting the value of your department into context. At the very least, they enable you to demonstrate whether your department is improving its productivity relative to the rest of the organisation. As you grow bolder, you may even choose to undertake comparisons with the outside market, but be careful if you do so. Unless the organisations chosen are very similar (as to industry, size and location in particular), you run the risk of reaching misleading conclusions.

The same definitions used in Chapter 1 can be re-applied, but with the following additions:

Human resource expenses (HRE) are the total operating expenses in the control of the HR department (i.e. remuneration of the team and cost of facilities or equipment used by them; training and staff-development budgets; research; IR; communications, etc).

Human resource headcount (HRH) is the total FTE establishment of the HR department at month-end.

Human resource costs (HRC)

This provides one of the most basic financial indicators of your department's efficiency. It is calculated by dividing the operating expenses of your department by the total operating expenses of the whole organisation:

$$HRC = \frac{HRE}{EX}.$$

The ratio is most commonly used for comparative purposes (see Figure 6), to identify trends and to justify demands when budgets are being set for the year.

It is even possible to introduce a productivity indicator by comparing HRC to the headcount of the organisation. In other words, divide HRC by HC, thereby demonstrating whether an improvement in HRC is better (or worse) than might have been expected due simply to changes in the population for which it holds budgets.

At a more subtle level, you can split the HRE element into your constituent budgets, thereby identifying the proportion of expenses that your department is *consuming* versus those you are *administering*, as shown in Figure 7.

You can even try this calculation several times, each time for different operating units, to see where the best (and worst) use of your resources is being made. For example, Figures 8a and b (see pp. 20/21) reveal that the Sales division has a worsening HRC and the Production division a virtually steady HRC. More important, Production has been steadily increasing training and reducing recruitment costs, whilst Sales appears to be spending a lot on training people who are replaced the next year.

The Business of People

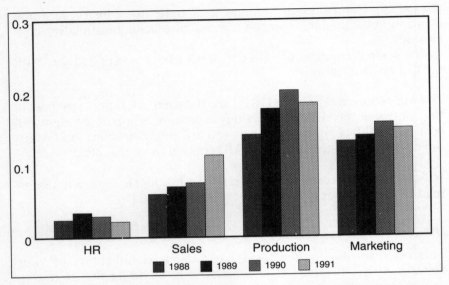

Figure 6   HRC Compared to Equivalents in Other Departments

Human Resource Ratio (HRR)

The other classic measure of the HR department is the ratio of its headcount to that of the total organisation:

$$HRR = \frac{HC}{HRH}.$$

This measurement has its roots in the belief that it is possible to determine how many people are ideally needed in one function to support a given number of people in another. Fortunately, perhaps, it is never that simple, since the range and depth of services *expected* will vary enormously over time and across organisations.

However, the extent and ambitiousness of an organisation's HR objectives will show up in this ratio, which may therefore be an indicator as to how attractive the environment will be to an HR professional – particularly when compared to others in the same industry. Targets are commonly expressed anywhere on a wide range between 50:1 and 200:1, with even more extreme values sometimes given. All that really matters is that you can spot trends and decide whether these are justified by external factors and the organisation's own intentions.

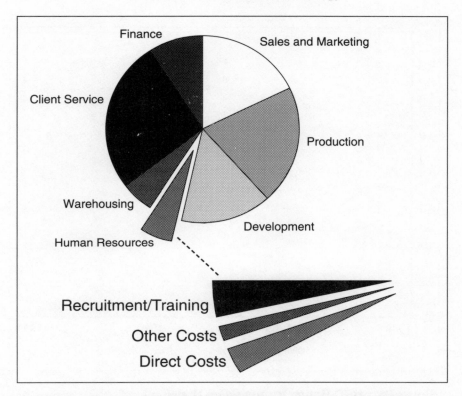

Figure 7   HRC – with HRE Subdivided into Constituent Budgets

Controlled Measurements

In addition to justifying your existence and general costs, you may well feel it would be useful to show that you understand the impact of the biggest cost indirectly associated with your department – the organisation's paybill. Although many special factors can result in dramatic changes to the paybill, over and above expected inflationary pressures, half the battle is simply being aware of the changes soon enough. The mere fact that the paybill is increasing is neither surprising nor very useful in itself.

Compensation Ratio (CR)

A comparison that is useful is the relative growth in paybill to all

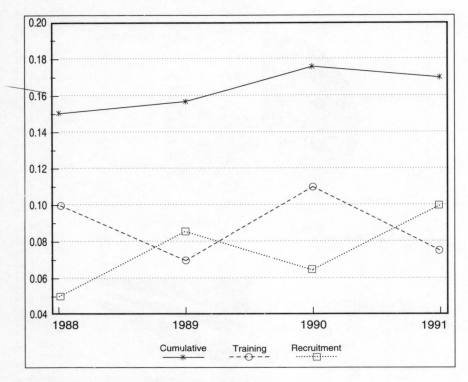

Figure 8a   HRC Ratios for the Sales Division

other operating expenses, calculated by dividing the total compensation/benefits bill by the organisation's operating costs:

$$CR = \frac{CO + BE}{EX}.$$

This shows the percentage of organisational costs that are directly related to employees. Deliberate changes in this ratio may be planned, of course, if you are investing in automation or providing a higher service content to your clients. In either case you can test whether the plans are being correctly implemented.

It can also be useful to do this calculation with and without particular benefits such as cars. This may help identify imbalances that are drifting into the total package, as can be seen in Figure 9, where car costs are rising out of proportion to employment and total costs.

It may also seem tempting to apply measures like this to individual departments, but great care is needed if you try. Unless you have *all*

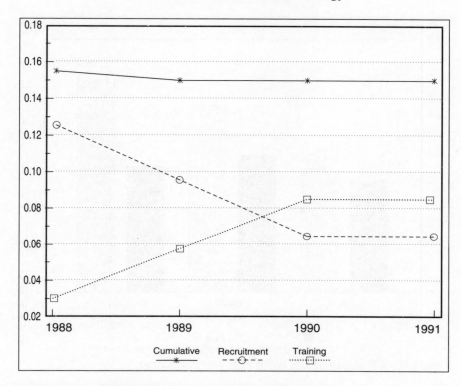

Figure 8b   HRC Ratios for the Production Division

the relevant factors for a particular department, your interpretation of the figures may be highly inaccurate (if some responsibilities were merged with another department, for instance). You should certainly never draw a direct comparison between departments; it would be like comparing strawberries to cream – they may go well together, but have little inherently in common.

So how can you influence and persuade your organisation to make the investments necessary to achieve their and your targets? Understanding the general financial perspective should help you speak the same language as other decision-makers. And you now have the basic figures to defend and justify the very existence of your department. Yet so far everything has revolved around historical data – monitoring but not necessarily planning any changes. In today's world that can never be enough since, as the cliché goes, the only constant is change.

For example, when your Managing Director asks: 'Why are our

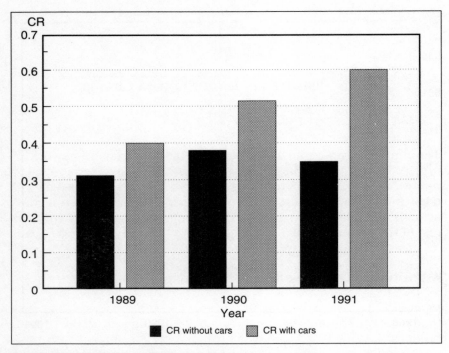

Figure 9   Changes in CR (with and without Cars)

employment costs higher than those of our competitors?' you need to
be able to quantify the areas to tackle. The impact of remuneration,
turnover, recruitment, training and more are all likely to be contributory factors, but which one (or combination) is your primary
problem?

If you want human resource decisions to be seen as truly strategic
in your organisation, your views need to gain the true credibility that
will come only with a general conviction that you understand their
financial implications. Once that goal has been reached you will be in
a stronger position to tackle the naivety shown by most other managers in human resource matters.

For instance, there is an all too common expectation by financially
trained people that productivity can be automatically increased by
spending more money on equipment; or that costs can be saved
simply by freezing recruitment. You may well know better, but find it
hard to demonstrate the consequences or illustrate the benefits of
any more appropriate actions. What are needed are joint measurements that mean the same thing to you and your colleagues and that
will allow you to plan together for change.

Chapter 3

Joint Measurements for Planned Change

The emphasis up to now has been on the financial framework of organisations, at least in so far as measurements involve personnel-related data. Yet if personnel is really to become an integral part of the strategy and not just a more effective influencer, then it must actually be able to formulate and implement plans jointly with the rest of the organisation.

A Position of Opportunity

In a sense, you have the potential for far greater impact on strategies than most other functions. Finance often concentrates on the presentation of historical facts (as well as managing the current cash position), whilst most other functions are focussed on the delivery of something unique to their department. In Personnel you are responsible for the human element of a range of strategies that span all aspects of the organisation.

Or, to look at it another way, Finance measures the past and tries to value the potential. Personnel should measure the potential, try to value the future and then plan to deliver it. Once it is realised that the most serious threat of competition is from the external market and not other departments, it is amazing how quickly old rivalries are swept aside and replaced by a determination to win together.

If such an enhanced global role for Personnel seems a little over-optimistic (IBM is seen as unusual in combining its Corporate Affairs and Personnel functions under one Director), then consider whether anyone else has a better chance to implement change. For all the attempts to separate visions from details, theorists from managers and planners from implementors, two essential points stand out: no plan is of any use unless it is implemented; and no-one, therefore, should accept responsibility for planning but not for execution. Although the obstacles to successful implementation are usually numerous, a common thread is the human factor. Not just at the individual level, but in terms of the wrong people being in the wrong place at the wrong time – or without sufficiently clear objectives, competent management or effective motivation.

You won't need telling that, although these are classic personnel issues, the most frequent obstacle to implementing effective strategies is also a people factor. The unwillingness of other managers or directors to pay more than lip service to investing in their staff, in an attempt to save time or money, is often described as being short-sighted. Indeed, this is quoted as a classic example of the Western predilection for the kind of 'short-termism' that tends to mitigate against any planned improvements in the longer run.

But could it be that we are simply not managing to quantify the effects of their support, or lack of it, in terms that they understand? Yes, this usually involves translating concepts that may seem esoteric outside Personnel into financial judgements and options. This is not the same as converting people into mere numbers, but it does provide an opportunity for you to communicate, in a globally understood language, decisions and plans that can change the whole future of your organisation and make your life more rewarding along the way.

Clarity of Intentions

Without launching into the subject of communications in any great depth, it is worth stating the apparently obvious at least once, since it is so often ignored. What you *intend* to communicate is unimportant; the crucial thing is what other people *perceive* you to have meant. And the results can often be far apart.

There is a no doubt apocryphal story of a well-meaning lady, travelling on British Rail, who felt that she should engage a rather taciturn traveller in conversation. As the train drew into a station he got up and left. A minute later, as the train started up again, the lady noticed his glasses on the seat and, rushing to the window, flung them at a passing porter with a brief description. Her inner glow from a deed well done, however, was shattered when the man re-appeared carrying the cup of tea that he had just bought in the dining-car.

Whilst hindsight, with or without glasses, is a rare commodity this story illustrates the dangers of confusing well-intentioned but ill-thought-out *activity* with proper objectives and plans. In a business environment, the essential need to focus on objectives not only aids faster and more effective implementation – it also facilitates monitoring of results and any necessary adaptations.

If Personnel is to continue its evolution from its fire-fighting, welfare traditions into a truly strategic role, then it not only needs to speak the language of business but to operate within its framework.

This is why so much comparison with competitors has been suggested earlier on.

The other key point is to be aware of the internal politics of communications. Although HR data is probably the least understood data in any organisation and is critical to strategic decisions, simply having the information is not enough. It is only when you can communicate it *to the format expected by other departments* that you will gain their respect and trust – so long as you also prove to be right more often than not. When you go overseas you will notice a marked increase in the respect with which you are treated if you even attempt the local language; the same applies at work.

Each department may have different objectives, but should share with you a common vision and infrastructure. If two people see the same object from different vantage points, their perceptions may well differ. Whilst this can be useful in the right circumstances, it can also cause much unnecessary confusion. So, whether you intend to provide proactive data in strategic areas or actually to generate the strategies themselves, take time to ensure that objectives and intentions are clearly understood by your colleagues – preferably in their terms.

The Competition Factor

Competitive advantage is essential for all organisations, private or public, in an increasingly global market. It must be the job of personnel to maximise the effective use of the organisation's human resources in order to maintain or increase this advantage. To achieve this demands a definition of where the actual, or potential, competitive advantage lies for your organisation.

Although this is a large topic in itself, such advantage is usually achieved through one of three types of approach. *Price leadership*, based on the minimalisation of costs, means using the experience of employees to improve efficiency. *Differentiation* of products or services tends to rely on the ability of staff to effect change quickly. A *niche market focus* will require you to add value relevant to that niche, usually based on outright innovation.

All of these strategic approaches mean that the organisation has to harness the creativity, enthusiasm and knowledge of its people, often as part of smaller business units. The information needed to achieve this is usually held by Personnel, but is often inaccessible – or ignored. If this is to change, then Personnel must gain the confidence of other functions through clarity of vision and the accuracy and timeliness of any data presented.

Valid Data Collection

Without wanting to go into too much tedious detail, there are a few worthwhile rules of data collection that mean you can concentrate on the more interesting bits. They can also be used as a starting point to develop your own ever more complex standards:

Rule 1. The different types of data must be clearly defined and understood, so that comparisons can be based on consistent assumptions.

Rule 2. All monitoring and reporting should take place at consistent intervals (unless attention is drawn to a deliberate exception), since trends can be badly misinterpreted otherwise.

Rule 3. All items of data should be entered into as few different reporting systems as possible, to avoid human error and loss of data integrity – where two systems purport to contain the same data but are not equally up-to-date.

Rule 4. All comparisons (and particularly with competitors) are affected by external factors. At least when comparisons are made within the organisation you can, and should, try to estimate the effect of any bias that these factors are having on the results.

All these rules, and any others you choose to add, apply whether you use manual or computer systems. The benefits of using computers come from automation of the procedures once they are set up, *not* from enabling you to avoid establishing the systems and their operating standards in the first place.

Due Statistical Caution

Particular care must be taken not to fall into the trap of ignoring your original objectives and searching the statistics for additional information that is unlikely to be valid. A cautionary example of this happened during World War II. In 1944 someone drew up a list of the leaders of the main warring nations and performed some calculations on 4 key factors – showing a remarkable coincidence:

	year of birth		age this year		year took office		years in office		Total
Churchill	1874	+	70	+	1940	+	4	=	3,888
Roosevelt	1882	+	62	+	1932	+	12	=	3,888
Stalin	1879	+	65	+	1924	+	20	=	3,888
Hitler	1889	+	55	+	1932	+	12	=	3,888
Mussolini	1883	+	61	+	1922	+	22	=	3,888

Fantastic predictions were made on the basis of this discovery, whilst totally ignoring the obvious. For *any* person, if you add the year in which they are born to their current age, you will get the current year. The same principle applies to the next two columns and, therefore, the total will not only always be identical but will have the 'magical' value of being twice the current year.

One other note of caution is not to stray into the realms of *forecasting* unless you understand a good deal of probability theory. A favourite exemplar of statisticians shows the danger. If a father says: 'At least one of my two children is a girl', what are the chances of the other child *also* being a girl? 99% per cent of people will respond 50:50 or 1 in 2. However, if there are two children one of whom is definitely a girl, then there are three possible and equally likely combinations (i.e. girl-girl, girl-boy or boy-girl – where the first of each pair is the elder child). The correct statistical forecast, therefore, is odds of only 33% (or 1 in 3) – much less likely than generally assumed.

You will gain the most value from the data available to you if you use it to communicate with those that think in terms of historic ratios and *to set and monitor the progress of plans*. Plans for achieving change, based on past results, are obviously recommended, but since these are rarely anchored in any theory of probability they should not be regarded as true forecasts.

Ideally you should be concentrating on opportunities for competitive advantage, rather than increasing or decreasing any ratios for their own sake. To do this properly means acquiring additional, freely available data relating to your competitors so that you can create benchmarks against which to measure the performance of your organisation. (Although this advice might seem targeted solely at the private sector, in practice all sectors are competing for skills and revenues/funding within their market.) Being competitive today means quickly reacting to change – or, better still, being there first – which requires accurate and timely personnel information on which to base quality decisions.

PART TWO:
A PRACTICAL ASSESSMENT

In the first part of this book attention has been given to the effectiveness of the organisation as a whole. Whilst I hope it has been useful and instructive in setting the financial framework in which we operate, it may seem a bit removed from the practical day-to-day activities of the Personnel department.

Today, there is much talk of changing cultures and structures. In particular, the emphasis has moved from hierarchical management to team motivation, from investment in materials to investment in knowledge, from a focus on production targets to service targets, and from measuring output to driving quality. Almost by definition these are very difficult concepts to quantify, yet it remains essential to find a way of measuring the results – and specifically the *changes* that can be attributed to any new policies.

If you have already built complex models of your organisation in order to achieve this, then this section – indeed this book – is probably not for you. You are also in a tiny, but laudable, minority at the vanguard of true integration of Personnel with business strategy. For the rest of us, a more realistic target is just to identify those activities in which we are involved where cost-effective change may be achieved.

This section of the book is designed to help you quickly and easily quantify these priorities and thereby support you in the planning process. It is rare that any area cannot achieve some improvement, but you still need to be able to focus on the problem areas first.

The emphasis in each chapter is always practical. The activity is broken down into key elements that can be measured simply by you. No targets are pre-set, since it is up to you to set objectives. Although examples are given, these are just to demonstrate methods of calculations and should not necessarily be seen as benchmarks.

In each case it is suggested that you start by performing the calculations on the most recently available data, such as the figures for the last financial year. If you then repeat the calculations, either for previous years or for major competitors, you should be able to identify the severity (or otherwise) of the particular problem.

More important, even if you end up having to concentrate on an area for reasons of political expediency or simply because you 'know'

29

it's the one to focus on, you at least have a benchmark against which to plan changes. An ability to keep monitoring the effects of your actions, by providing a constant set of reference points, is the only way to ensure that common standards of quality are maintained throughout. As you complete each exercise you are giving yourself one more piece of information with which to refine future decisions and improve your chances of success.

The frequency with which you review your data and assess trends is particularly important. If it is too infrequent, you may see things too late and find that you are merely reporting on history, not identifying opportunities for change. On the other hand, too frequent analysis may appear to indicate trends that don't really exist. The most appropriate frequency, therefore, will vary for each topic and is best found by trial and error.

A useful exercise can be to try more than one frequency and then overlay the results. This may show cyclical trends that indicate additional factors that should be considered when assessing the impact of planned changes. Remember that if a picture is worth a thousand words, then so is relevant data – when correctly summarised. Just because you have collected vast volumes of data in analysing a particular problem area does not mean that anyone else wants to see it. But if the problem is clearly quantified, trends identified and a performance measurement shown, then most people will listen to your proposals.

These chapters can be tackled in any order. Indeed you can ignore those that you believe to be either irrelevant or fully under control in your organisation. You can also adapt them, if you feel this would be helpful, but should take care to keep them consistent for comparative purposes.

Chapter 4

Less Absent Resources

Whether or not you make allowances for it in your headcount plans, if you pay for employees who are late for work or don't turn up at all you are not getting what you pay for. This is not a problem that can be fully eradicated, since some unplanned absences may be fully justified and authorised. However, many absences (in some industries, the majority) are *not* authorised and these cost your organisation dearly.

Did you know that unplanned absence from work in the UK costs at least 40 times more, per annum, than industrial action? Rather more important, do you know your organisation's total costs for absent staff last year, by staff and by department? And can you identify likely causes and cures?

We have all heard speeches with jokes based on the reasons submitted for absences. Since many are longer than the average shaggy dog I will not repeat them here, but in most cases the main point is being missed. Whether the individual excuse is amusing or not, far more creativity is being expended on it than on identifying and reducing the underlying causes. If your organisation has a formal policy that allows and therefore gives credence to an expected level of unauthorised absenteeism, then it had better be able to explain why it can afford to waste this money rather than invest it in training or elsewhere.

This may sound harsh, but paying for non-productive resources is pointless if it can be avoided. Whilst levels of productivity will be influenced by skill, culture and management factors, it cannot make sense to accept that you will sometimes be paying for zero output. The best way to understand the scope of opportunity that may be available to your organisation is first to quantify the scale of the costs involved.

Costing Absenteeism

- The UK average for unplanned and unauthorised absences from

31

work is about 7% of the total time available, although it is much higher in some industries
- In an organisation of 500 employees, a 7% absence rate is equivalent to 8,225 days lost per year – or over *16 days per person per year*
- Given an average wage cost of £250 per week, the cost of this absenteeism is some *£411,250* p.a. on a paybill of £6.5 million.

This, of course, is only the direct cost; the hidden costs of absenteeism also include:

- permanent overstaffing to cover the expected level of absenteeism
- temporary workers and/or overtime to cover additional unexpected absences
- the cost of supervisory time in attempting to deal with the problem
- the impact on morale if absenteeism is allowed to remain unchecked.

Even without these substantial costs being added, the scale of resources being wasted is frankly staggering. It is often at least 2 to 3 times more than the training budget and may even represent the difference between profit and loss.

Now imagine that you have identified procedures that may require some initial investment but should lead to a reduction in the absenteeism rate. An effective computerised system, for example, can provide accurate monitoring of the data and give line managers the confidence to take appropriate action. This has been found typically to produce a reduction in absenteeism of around 4 days per person per year in many industries. If applied in the case given earlier, this 2% reduction (i.e. from 7% to 5%) would generate a direct saving of *£117,500* every year – without even attempting to calculate the indirect savings. Looked at like this, your request for investment may well seem attractive.

BASE ASSUMPTIONS used in the above calculations are:

Number of full-time employees	= 500
Number of working days p.a.	= 235
Average weekly wage	= £250
Current absenteeism rate	= 7%
Reduction in absenteeism rate	= 2%

In order to relate these calculations to your own organisation, you need to define the items that you are measuring. For the purposes of this book it is assumed that the definition given earlier still applies for headcount; the following are also used:

Workdays = the average number of days available for work (i.e. excluding authorised absences such as holidays) for the period in question.

Wages = the average contractual weekly compensation for all employees, excluding overtime.

Absenteeism = any non-scheduled absences, i.e. not for holidays or training but including sickness, jury service, etc.

As most of this data should be fairly accessible, you can now calculate what absenteeism is costing your organisation and what the value of any savings that you can achieve would be.

Sample Form for Calculation

Cost of absenteeism

Enter number of employees _____ (a),
Enter average weekly wage £ _____ (b),
Multiply (a) x (b) £ _____ (c),
Multiply (c) x 52 £ _____ = Total paybill

Enter total absence days p.a. _____ (d),
Enter number of working days p.a. _____ (e),
Divide [(d) x 100] by [(a) x (e)] _____ % (f) = Absenteeism rate

Multiply [(b)/5] x (d) £ _____ (g) = Absenteeism cost p.a.

Potential cost saving

Enter saving in absent days p.a. _____ (h),
Divide (h) by (d) _____ (i),
Multiply (i) x (g) £ _____ = Total savings p.a.

You may now choose, if you have the data, to repeat this exercise on sub-sets of the data for various grades or departments. If you do so, remember that your original objective was to identify the scale of the problem and to monitor the effect of new measures – not to create a competitive league table for its own sake. The best way to achieve

Cost of Different Absenteeism Rates							
1%		2%		5%		10%	
1990 £	1991 £	1990 £	1991 £	1990 £	1991 £	1990 £	1991 £
Department							
Prod – Ldn							
4700	4061	9400	8122	23500	20304	47000	40608
Prod – Man 5875	8883	11750	17766	29375	44415	58750	88830
Prod – Cov 9400	6091	18800	12182	47000	30456	94000	60912
Whse – Man 902	1946	1805	3892	4512	9729	9024	19458
Whse – Cov 1805	973	3610	1946	9024	4865	18048	9729
Sale – Sth 2187	2577	4374	5155	10935	12887	21869	25775
Sale – Mid 1193	1074	2386	2148	5964	5370	11929	10740
Sale – Nth 1392	1718	2783	3437	6958	8592	13917	17183
Serv – S/E 1624	1462	3249	2923	8122	7309	16243	14617
Serv – S/W 812	877	1624	1754	4061	4385	8122	8770
Serv – Mid 1354	1316	2707	2631	6768	6578	13536	13155
Serv – N/W 948	1169	1895	2339	4738	5847	9475	11694
Serv – N/E 812	877	1624	1754	4061	4385	8122	8770
Admn – H/O 2846	2285	5692	4570	14229	11426	28459	22851
Total 35850	35309	71699	70619	179247	176548	358494	353092

Notes: Average headcount decreased by 10% from 1990 to 1991.
Average wage-rate increased   by 8% from 1990 to 1991.
Total wage-bill decreased by 1.5% from 1990 to 1991.

Average cost of absence per day is virtually unchanged. If redundancies in 1991 are accompanied by increased absence-rates, then the cost of absenteeism will be higher than in 1990 – despite the lower headcount.

Figure 10   Savings Potential by Department

this is to set up a spreadsheet to make the calculations shown in the previous framework (with your own amendments if you prefer). This can then be used to generate reports, such as those shown below.

The first report (Figure 10) simply lists all departments, showing the cost for each that would have been incurred had various absenteeism rates applied over the last two years. This can be used to identify the areas with greatest potential that are worthy of a closer look. The second report (Figure 11) incorporates targets and current data, so that the effect of intended preventative action – and its results – can be clearly shown.

As always in this book, it is assumed that you have the means to acquire and store relevant data in the first place (whether manually

Department	Actual 1990 £	Actual 1991 £	Target 1992 Q1 £	Target 1992 Q2 £	Actual 1992 Q1 £	Actual 1992 Q2 £	Variance 1992 Q1 £	Variance 1992 Q2 £
Prod – Ldn	37130	35329	8633	8107	8212	—	421	—
Prod – Man	37013	61293	14739	13588	14970	—	(231)	—
Prod – Cov	127840	88932	22267	21477	18950	—	3317	—
Whse – Man	5505	13037	3133	2880	2930	—	203	—
Whse – Cov	22921	13523	3385	3259	2905	—	480	—
Sale – Sth	7435	9537	2143	1808	2009	—	134	—
Sale – Mid	6441	6336	1507	1367	1340	—	167	—
Sale – Nth	5288	7045	1607	1384	1384	—	223	—
Serv – S/E	14781	14617	3605	3416	3340	—	265	—
Serv – S/W	4954	5876	1412	1298	1321	—	91	—
Serv – Mid	11235	11971	2938	2767	2835	—	103	—
Serv – N/W	4548	6081	1427	1275	1245	—	182	—
Serv – N/E	5035	5964	1435	1321	1366	—	69	—
Admn – H/O	29881	26279	6553	6255	6136	—	417	—
Total	320007	305820	74784	70202	68943	—	5841	—

Notes: No change in headcount from 1991 to 1992.
Average wage-rate increased by 4% from 1991 to 1992.
Unchanged absence-rates would cost £318,053 during 1992.
Absence-rates targeted to reduce by 0.5% per quarter in 1992.

It can be shown that achieving the plan would generate savings of £4,730 in quarter 1;
£9,311 in quarter 2;
£18,329 in quarter 3;
£36,081 in quarter 4.

Savings achieved after first quarter = a quarter of the annual 'unchanged' rate (£318,053) minus the actual rate = £10,570 (223% of plan).

Figure 11   Savings Planned and Achieved

or on computer). The system that you use for this purpose should hold far greater detail for each person, such as the frequency, reason and duration of absences – so that patterns of absence behaviour can be identified and corrective action introduced.

For instance, it is generally accepted that certain factors tend to contribute to higher rates of absenteeism – such as the distance travelled to work each day. Since such correlation can be expected (if not accepted), it often makes more sense to target areas of high absenteeism where this is *not* an apparent contributory factor.

Another good example is mapping absence patterns in your organisation against the days of the week. Various surveys have found that absence across a wide range of industries occurs 50–60% of the time on Mondays and/or Fridays. Since a certain percentage of those absences must be unjustified, a team with a particularly poor record on these two days merits closer attention.

It has also been noted, unsurprisingly enough, that a considerable worsening of an individual's absence record often presages their leaving the organisation. Whilst this can be cause and effect (i.e. being fired for poor attendance), it is extremely common even when the employee resigns voluntarily. Given the attendant replacement costs, the opportunity to use absence records to identify problems can have a double cost benefit.

However, we are not concerned here with effecting these changes, but with understanding the severity and location of the problem. It should be possible to set a target for improvement, quantify how much it is worth spending on the exercise and then monitor the overall effectiveness and payback achieved.

For instance, you may decide to separate out absences by the duration of each one. This will generate somewhat unwieldy volumes of data, but you can consolidate this into more basic information for each department, as shown in Figure 12. In this kind of analysis, care should be taken to use *the number of absences* of a particular duration, not the number of *days* consumed in each case. The latter will show a much higher apparent preponderance of lengthy absences, but will be distorted by the size of a few major absences.

In the example shown, Location A has a fairly typical profile, where around 50% of absences are of 3 days or less, and well over two-thirds are under 6 days. Location B appears to be suffering from the 'self-certification' syndrome: morale is so low that when a person is off sick it becomes tempting to extend it to 2 or 3 days without hassle.

Location C, however, may look more puzzling – with a substantial blip of 5-day absences on an otherwise normal profile, which may indicate that a local GP is prone to issuing certificates without care. This does happen. I once visited the doctor to collect a prescription for a friend and the first question I was asked was: 'Well, how many days off do you want?' After explaining the true situation, I enquired why he was so ready to tailor the certificate to the demands of the patient.

The explanation was simple. The average GP is concerned to reduce his or her caseload, in order to provide a responsive service when needed. If a patient wants 4 days off and is only given a certificate for 3 days, they tend to come back on the fourth day to ask

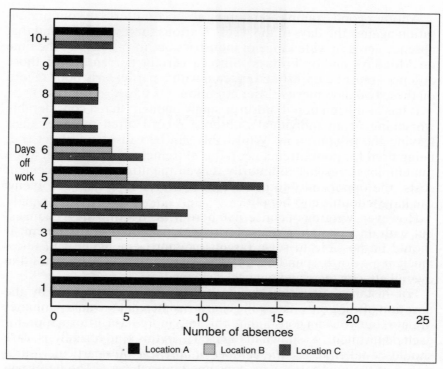

Figure 12   Occurrences of Absence – by Duration

again. So, by acquiescing in their original demand, the GP saves time and reduces the queue for others. Some unscientific research has unveiled the claim that over a third of all prescriptions written by GPs are never presented at the pharmacist's. Making it easy to take a week off can unfortunately prove equally irresistible to both over-worked and lazy staff. Distinguishing one from the other, however, is not usually too difficult, once you have identified the affected group.

Finally, it may also be valid to compare your rate of absenteeism with that of your competitors – if you can obtain the figures. If you can't, you can still probably hazard a fairly accurate estimate from experience. The point is not necessarily to achieve cost savings. If your absenteeism rate is 7% but your competitors typically average 15%, then you can probably afford to tackle other issues first. If, however, their rate is only 3% and yours is still 7%, you need to address the problem quickly – before the wasted money makes it even harder to free up the budgets for training or recruitment that will be necessary to continue competing.

Chapter 5

Reducing Turnover Costs

Labour turnover seems to be one of those topics that is always fashionable, although its relevance and interpretation vary widely. When the skills shortage is considered the central focus of most personnel strategies, retention of staff is regarded as critical. When restructuring and downsizing are more in evidence, you will hear that resignations should be seen as an opportunity to evaluate whether a job needs refilling anyway.

There is certainly a valid argument that wastage fuels the HR plan and should not be eradicated, since the dynamics that result have some positive impact on career development and the acquisition of skills. However, the reality of labour turnover is that *it can never be desirable in itself* since it represents an investment that is leaving for good. The degree of harm relates very closely to whether it is the individual or the organisation that has decided to part company with the other. After all, if the organisation plans to do without an individual (or their job), then the decision ought to have been thoroughly costed and justified.

If this is not the case, then the effect will be much the same as when the organisation is the last to know that an individual is leaving of their own accord. Even without taking account of the undoubted overmanning which is still built in to many organisations as protection against uncontrolled labour turnover, the costs are far more severe than many realise.

Did you know that the real costs of staff turnover equate to an *average 6 months' salary* (and up to 2 years' depending on the job) for each leaver, before effective replacement is achieved? Do you have succession plans for key jobs, and a developing pool of talent for most functions, that will allow for their learning curve? Can you account for management time spent on selection, as well as direct advertising or agency fees?

Even if a job is refilled by an internal transfer, all the above problems and costs will simply be moved elsewhere. The costs, which are often not acknowledged, include:

38

- *immediate cover* provided by temporary staff, or by overtime payments, during the replacement period
- *interviewing time* spent by line managers, supervisors and the Personnel department
- *direct recruitment* costs of advertising and/or agency fees
- *induction training* materials and trainers for new employees
- *non-productive* salary for new employees during their learning curve
- *continuing cover* by temporary staff, or overtime payments, during the learning curve.

Even without trying to account for the knock-on effect that high turnover has on morale and hence productivity, or to value the loss of undocumented knowledge, it can be quickly demonstrated that unplanned turnover has a cost that *no organisation can honestly afford*.

Costing Labour Turnover

- Many organisations experience a turnover in staff of 20% p.a. (and even more in certain industries). Very few manage to achieve a level below 10%.
- In an organisation of 500 employees, a 10% turnover rate obviously means *50 staff lost in a year*.
- Given an average wage cost of £250 per week, the typical cost of labour turnover is some *£359,950* on a paybill of £6.5 million.

Unless you hold detailed labour turnover data for your organisation, it is next to impossible to derive useful inputs for HR planning processes. Ideally you should also be able to separate out voluntary and involuntary terminations. Focussing on such key data, through its administration on a computer system for instance, will enable you to identify the areas of greatest labour turnover and to analyse the underlying reasons. The savings that result can be dramatic.

If you manage to reduce the labour turnover rate by at least 2% in the above example (i.e. from 10% to 8%), this would mean a direct saving of *£71,990 p.a.* An effective system might also enable you to start any recruitment earlier or increase the speed of processing applications. In either case, if the result is an average decrease in recruitment time of at least 20%, then you would generate a further direct saving of *£18,750 p.a.* Focussing on key positions may enable you to achieve even greater savings.

BASE ASSUMPTIONS used in the above calculations are:

Number of full-time employees	= 500
Number of working days p.a.	= 235
Average weekly wage	= £250
Temporary staff/overtime rates	= 1.5 × wage-rate
Average manager weekly wage	= £375
Average staff replacement time	= 25 days
Average preparation/interviewing time	= 0.5 days per applicant
Number of applicants shortlisted	= 3 per position
Average recruitment costs/fees	= 17.5% of annual salary
New employee induction training	= 2 days
Frequency of induction training	= 2 days every month
Learning curve productive contribution	= 3 months @ 50%
Current labour turnover rate	= 10%
Reduction in labour turnover rate	= 2%
Reduction in replacement time	= 20%

All of these assumptions can be replaced by your own figures, but one in particular may need some explanation. The figure given for the 'learning curve productive contribution' assumes that, on average, a new employee is only operating at 25% productivity in their first month, at 50% in the second and at 75% in the third. In this case the total for the three-month period equals 50%, but you may well find very different averages for different jobs in your organisation. You can now calculate what this aspect of labour turnover is directly costing your organisation and what the value of any savings that you can achieve would be.

As a starting point, before delving into so many calculations, you may wish to establish some basic ratios for turnover in your organisation in order to identify the areas requiring the most urgent attention. Labour turnover is generally quantified by taking the number of leavers (for any given period) and dividing this by the average number of employees over the same period. The problem is that few people can agree on what the average figure for employees really represents. For instance, if you have high turnover, the headcount will vary widely during the period measured – depending on the success of re-recruitment at each moment. The ratio also takes no account of deliberate changes in overall headcount, such as rapid growth. For instance, if you are regularly losing 20% of your staff p.a. but increase your headcount this year by 30% through additional recruitment, the labour turnover ratio would appear as just under 17.5% rather than 20% – despite the fact that you have lost the same number of staff as before.

Sample Form for Calculation

Costing labour turnover

Enter number of employees	_____ (a),
Enter average weekly wage	£ _____ (b),
Multiply (a) x (b)	£ _____ (c),
Multiply (c) x 52	£ _____ (d) = Total paybill
Enter current turnover rate	___%___ (e),
Multiply (e) x (a)	_____ (f) = Staff loss p.a.
Enter average number of days to replace	_____ (g)
Multiplier rate for overtime/temps.	_____ (h),
Multiply (b) x (h)	£ _____ (i),
Multiply (f) x (g) x [(i)/5]	£ _____ (j) = Immediate cover costs
Preparation and interview time per applicant (days)	_____ (k),
Shortlisted applicants per position	_____ (l),
Enter average manager weekly wage	£ _____ (m),
Multiply (f) x (k) x (l) x [(m)/5]	£ _____ (n) = Interview time costs
Enter average recruitment fees	___%___ (o),
Multiply (d) x (e) x (o)	£ _____ (p) = Recruitment fee costs
Length of induction training (days)	_____ (q),
Frequency of this training (p.a.)	_____ (r),
Multiply [(b)/5] x (q) x [(f)+(r)]	£ _____ (s) = Induction training cost
Duration of learning curve (months)	_____ (t),
Enter non-productive element	___%___ (u),
Multiply (d) x (e) x [(t)/12] x (u)	£ _____ (v) = Non-productive costs
Multiply (t) x (u) (months)	_____ (w),
Multiply (d) x (e) x (h) x [(w)/12]	£ _____ (x) = Continuing cover costs
Multiply (g) x [(b)/5] x (f)	£ _____ (y) = Salary savings
Add (j)+(n)+(p)+(s)+(v)+(x) – (y)	£ _____ (z) = Turnover cost p.a.

Potential cost saving

Enter expected turnover reduction	___%___ (1),
Multiply (z) x [(1)/(e)]	£ _____ (2) = Labour turnover savings
Enter reduction in replacement time	___%___ (3),
Multiply (j) x (3)	£ _____ (4) = Added cover savings
Add (2) + (4)	£ _____ (5) = Total savings p.a.

Given the number of variables, it is not surprising that there are almost as many variant ratios for measuring labour turnover as the number of people trying to measure it. One that is particularly worth considering is often referred to as the *stability ratio*.

To derive this, you need first to calculate the length of service (LOS) for all people employed during the period concerned – usually a calendar year or quarter. You can then work out stability ratios for groups of employees, showing the relative stability for those with different lengths of employment. The calculation is simply the number of employees with greater than (say) 1 year's service divided by the headcount in place 1 year ago. An example of the kind of report that could be generated using these ratios is shown in Figure 13.

Report run in January 1992			
	LOS>1 year	*LOS>2 years*	*LOS>5 years*
Design Dept.			
London	0.833	0.727	0.400
Manchester	0.875	0.857	0.500
Production			
Slough	0.875	0.833	0.625
Uxbridge	0.933	0.917	0.636
Solihull	0.933	0.889	0.515
Redditch	0.698	0.692	0.375
Bury	0.909	0.429	0.389
Stores Units			
Team 1	0.824	0.750	0.500
Team 2	0.833	0.750	0.458
Team 3	0.895	0.833	0.636
Team 4	1.000	1.000	0.750
Team 5	0.875	0.833	0.458
Average	*0.874*	*0.792*	*0.520*

Notes: 20% redundancies declared in all Stores teams in 1988.
Overall headcount increased by 8% from 1986 to 1989.
Overall headcount increased by 24% during 1990.

Comment: Significant variances for Redditch (LOS>1) and Bury (LOS>2).

Figure 13   Stability Ratios by Length of Service

It is clear that the Production teams in Redditch and Bury are worth investigating, for very different reasons. At Bury, although nearly all of the employees have been there for more than 1 year, very few have an LOS greater than 2. If you don't already know the reason for this it might be a good idea to find out quickly. At Redditch, the picture is more confused. With a respectable ratio for LOS>2 years, why is it so bad for LOS>1 year and again for LOS>5 years? Are the two scores due to a repeating factor or totally unconnected? Again, a check is in order.

A clue might be gained by identifying and comparing the ratios for voluntary and involuntary leavers. This involves clearly distinguishing between the two categories, which should be easy but often leads to confusion through inconsistent definitions. (For instance, early retirement is usually considered to be voluntary whilst death is obviously involuntary.) I would prefer, therefore, to categorise leavers into those whose departure is instigated by the organisation (planned) and those who initiate the process themselves (volunteer). (Those who die in service probably need not be reported on at all.) At the very least, this will give you an indication as to the degree of control that the organisation maintains over turnover; an example appears in Figure 14.

With a little more effort, and the use of a spreadsheet to perform some of the calculations shown in the basic model, it is also possible to look at a breakdown of the types of cost incurred. This can allow you to evaluate alternative methods that might lead to savings merely by shifting the proportion between two sets of activities. For instance, you may consider allowing a greater proportion of the selection process to be handled by an external agency but be unsure as to whether this will prove too costly.

The kind of report which shows alternative scenarios based on different assumptions (see Figure 15) is very popular – but often for the wrong reasons. It is helpful in assessing the relative merits of alternative approaches, but in no way predicts a particular outcome – since it is entirely dependent on the accuracy of your assumptions. In other words, it is a working tool to aid your decisions, not an official forecast which relieves you of responsibility for the eventual result.

Another aspect of how you can keep adding to the model you have built of labour turnover costs is when you consider the indirect costs – or the consequential costs – of the turnover. This is an enormously complicated area and probably not worth trying to quantify too accurately at the first attempt, but the scope is dramatic. For instance, one fairly substantial direct cost has already been mentioned: the resources used when covering a vacant post until recruitment and induction have been completed.

But what about the increased likelihood of errors being made during that time – either through lack of essential skills or knowledge,

	1990 (Actual)		1991 (Actual)		1992 (Target)	
Percentages	Volunt.	Planned	Volunt.	Planned	Volunt.	Planned
Design Dept.						
London	10.5	3.8	3.4	4.3	5.9	5.1
Manchester	8.8	3.7	5.8	5.6	5.5	5.5
Production						
Slough	13.9	2.8	11.9	3.7	7.7	3.3
Uxbridge	3.6	3.1	5.0	2.4	6.4	4.6
Solihull	4.5	2.2	5.2	2.9	6.6	4.4
Redditch	21.5	9.3	6.9	6.1	5.8	5.2
Bury	6.7	2.4	8.9	4.2	8.2	2.8
Stores Units						
Team 1	11.8	4.9	11.2	12.3	6.8	4.2
Team 2	5.4	2.9	5.9	7.7	6.1	4.9
Team 3	12.6	4.1	14.8	11.9	7.1	3.9
Team 4	0.0	0.0	11.4	10.8	6.3	4.7
Team 5	5.1	3.2	2.3	6.8	5.9	5.1
Average	*8.7*	*3.5*	*7.7*	*6.6*	*6.5*	*4.5*

Notes: The 1991 total ratio (14.3%) is higher than for 1990 (12.2%), despite the lower number of leavers, due to the reduction in overall headcount by just over 10% during the year.

Comment: The planned element is up from 29% of the total in 1990 to 46% in 1991 – clearly showing the shift away from voluntary leavers. It is targeted to reduce this proportion in 1992, but only slightly.

Figure 14   Labour Turnover Ratios – Volunteer and Planned

or simply through any lesser commitment shown by temporary staff? In many functions the cost of such mistakes could exceed all the other costs combined. A misdirected or lost order, incorrect invoicing, wrong materials used, defective production – these and many similar problems have a habit of becoming more frequent during temporary cover, and can all be extremely costly. To some extent this is a quality issue, but labour turnover will certainly not improve it.

Finally, as always, it will be particularly useful if you can obtain some data on competitor organisations for comparative purposes. It is, ultimately, this measure that will make clear the importance of focussing your energies on this topic rather than another.

Requirement: to recruit 8 software programmers with different skill
profiles, to replace a team that will not relocate with
business unit

Critical   needed to start within 3 months;
factors: skill requirements cannot be lowered;
                  limited recruitment budget and resources

Scenario 1:   direct advertising campaign, with minimal reliance on
                  ad-hoc responses from agencies

Scenario 2:   project sub-contracted to agency, with only final selection
                  and offer stages retained in-house

	Scenario 1 £	Scenario 2 £	Variance £
Immediate cover	70,720	56,576	14,144
Advertisement, etc.	9,800	4,950	4,850
Admin/processing	3,692	308	3,384
Agency fees	10,350	18,400	(8,050)
Interviewing time	1,615	862	753
Sub-total	*96,177*	*81,096*	*15,081*

Conclusion: Even if immediate cover costs are excluded, it should still be
cheaper to try scenario 2.

Figure 15   Costs of Alternative Recruitment Methods

Chapter 6

Wastage and Replacement

'Wastage' by its very name, appears to imply something that is to be avoided. 'Labour turnover', on the other hand, is often seen as totally unavoidable. Despite the terms often being regarded as interchangeable, this apparent contradiction exists because few organisations bother to analyse either properly and so have a poor understanding of their situation. It is all too common to hear figures such as '*c.* 8% p.a.' being used to describe a company's labour turnover rate.

On its own, this kind of assessment is not only virtually meaningless but of no practical use. Wastage is the result of other factors, which can only be measured as more or less desirable if they are first identified and understood. Furthermore, it is not just the volume of leavers that matters, but their quality and the dependency of others on them. To take an extreme case, you may be happy to see a wastage rate of 30% p.a. in an area targeted for cutbacks, but distraught at a rate of 10% p.a. at a greenfield site receiving massive investment.

Changing external factors also play a part. During the late 1980s, all the talk was of the skills shortage and the need to retain staff, almost without regard to their contribution. In the computer sector, where retention had always been a problem, IBM was often held in awe for its ability to hold and grow staff. In addition to high-quality training and development facilities, this stability was no doubt assisted by an openly declared policy of no redundancies. In the early 1990s, however, their traditional approach came under intense pressure.

This was because an already low staff turnover rate all but dried up and, at the same time, the mean age of staff was increased as fewer new (young) staff were offered employment. Such a combination had dramatic implications for IBM's future and led executives to introduce innovative strategies to tempt many more senior staff to leave the fold voluntarily. Whilst no-one is gloating, this represented an expensive turnaround in attitudes towards wastage.

Although we have already measured the direct costs incurred through staff turnover in chapter 5, it is worth looking a little more closely at how to plan for managed wastage and thus minimise costs of replacements that are avoidable. It is worth emphasising that wastage refers here only to employees who *leave* the organisation – not to those who are promoted or transferred to a different post. Unlike labour turnover, therefore, it is not directly related to changes or growth in organisational structure of any type.

Many organisations keep records of the reasons given by employees who resign of their own accord. The problem is these are by their very nature subjective statements that do not lend themselves to accurate coding for the purpose of analysis. It is still worth doing, however, if only because it may occasionally reveal a specific and local problem – such as sexual harassment or formalised pilfering – that needs to be tackled immediately.

However, although you may have obtained a broad indication of the size of the wastage problem, reported individual factors will usually help you little on their own. What you are faced with is very similar to the actuarial problems with which insurers wrestle – not how to eradicate accidents (or, in this case, wastage), but how to reduce the risk of its happening to your population (or staff). The key to achieving this lies in identifying the sub-groups most at risk and then understanding the factors impacting on them.

Unfortunately, grouping 'high-risk' employees can be a bit hit and miss at first, because of the enormous number of ways in which they can be segmented, including any combination of one or more of the following:

age	qualifications
experience/skills	remuneration
length of service	job grade
department/division	location
contract type	gender
occupational category	ethnic origin
performance ratings	external change.

This is an example of where a computer can provide invaluable help. If all this basic information is held on a system, then it should not be difficult to generate multiple reports on the incidence of wastage – selecting a different combination of factors until you can see where the greatest correlation lies. Once these priority groupings have been identified, you at least have a target population on which to practise risk management.

You also have a list of *correlating* factors, although these must not be confused with causal factors (i.e. the *reasons* behind decisions to leave). So you may now know, for example, that whilst your average wastage rate in the company is 6% p.a., there is a rate of 35% amongst male trainee depot managers in the East Anglia region. This means you not only can place a cost on the general problem but can identify the potential for a specific saving, which often helps you gain approval in tackling the problem even if new investment is required.

Costing Wastage and Replacement

- Even if only the costs related to re-recruitment are taken into account, the increased frequency of the process leads to dramatic costs. The organisation used throughout this book could save *£66,000* p.a. simply by reducing the wastage rate amongst its East Anglian male trainee depot managers to the company average – and increasing their average LOS by 25% or 9 months.
- If there is an accompanying increase in morale and an improvement in the quality of hires, then the duration of both unfilled vacancies and of learning curves may reduce. These could add *a further £6,000 p.a.* to the identifiable savings available.
- Actual savings of even half of this total sum (£72,000 p.a.) would easily justify a one-off investment of, say, £24,000.

BASE ASSUMPTIONS used in the above calculations are:

Number of relevant employees	= 20
Average weekly wage	= £300
Average wastage rate	= 35%
Current average length of service	= 36 months
External recruitment costs and fees	= 15% annual salary
Area personnel total costs p.a.	= £50,000
Personnel time spent on recruitment	= 70%
Current time for unfilled vacancies	= 25 days
Temporary staff/overtime rates	= 1.5 × wage-rate
Current skills training per starter	= 45 days
Average cost of skills training	= £80 per day
Current learning curve duration	= 60 days
Average learning curve non-productivity	= 60%
Reduced wastage rate	= 6%
Increased average length of service	= 9 months
Reduced time for unfilled vacancies	= 5 days
Reduced skills training per starter	= 5 days
Reduced learning curve duration	= 10 days

Using a model similar to the one for calculating the total cost of labour turnover but applying only the statistics relating to the particular target group, it is easy to demonstrate the potential in each case (see p. 50).

However, this doesn't tell you what problem you are trying to tackle. Any scope for influencing potential wastage has been missed by the time of replacement and must be tackled at the initial point of selection. Most research claims that there are only two generally reliable indicators of wastage, over and above any major change enforced by the organisation itself – market-based (economic/skills) factors and age/length of service (LOS). However, as little can be done about these, this seems unduly defeatist.

It would take that rare beast, a professional econometrician, to build an effective model of the labour market, with all the complex relationships between international economics, national demographics and local skill factors for each occupational group. It is also likely that the result would be simply an academic exercise, offering more scope for argument about possible interpretations of the data than any useful plans.

But it is important not to give up at this point. Common sense will show that a few basic indicators are easily accessible, from local unemployment rates to transnational salary surveys. These are the market-based factors that enable employees wishing to leave actually to do so – or else restrict their choice. It is not absolute values that matter, but the correlation between them; unemployment and wastage rates, for example, tend to be inversely related. Whilst you may not be able easily to change this type of factor, you can make sure that you know which groups of employees are most at risk – i.e. have the motivation to leave, whether or not the opportunity yet exists.

Although it is worthwhile cross-tabulating the data in order to identify any factors specific to your organisation (or a department or location), there is one correlation that you are certain to find. Age and LOS are often regarded as closely linked with each other, mostly because so many organisations unfortunately still single out youth as a prime determinant in their selection criteria. As well as being short-sighted for the organisation itself, this exaggerates the natural tendency of younger employees to greater mobility – through an imbalance of market supply and demand that typically balances out only for those in their late 30s or 40s. Broadening the age range in recruitment can often be an option worth considering.

Why go through all this work if the ability to directly reduce the wastage appears so limited? There are two main reasons. First, many options *are* still open to you, from redefining job structures, changing your selection criteria, moving location, changing contract terms, etc. And, second, because accurate wastage data for each part of the organisation is essential if you wish to attempt any planning of future demand for recruitment or training.

As with all the chapters in this book, it is essential that any data you

Sample Form for Calculation

Costing wastage and replacement

Enter number of employees	_____ (a),	
Enter average weekly wage	£ _____ (b),	
Multiply (a) x (b)	£ _____ (c),	
Multiply (c) x 52	£ _____ (d)	= *Total paybill*
Enter current wastage rate	_____ % (e),	
Enter average recruitment fees	_____ % (f),	
Multiply (d) x (e) x (f)	£ _____ (g),	
Enter annual personnel staff costs	£ _____ (h),	
Enter % time spent on recruitment	_____ % (i),	
Multiply (h) x (i) and add (g)	£ _____ (j)	= *Administrative costs*
Enter average vacancy duration (days)	_____ (k),	
Multiplier rate for overtime/temps.	_____ (l),	
Multiply (b) x (l)	£ _____ (m),	
Multiply (a) x (e) x (k) x [(m)/5]	£ _____ (n)	= Unfilled vacancy costs
Enter skills training per starter (days)	_____ (o),	
Enter daily cost of skills training	£ _____ (p),	
Multiply (a) x (e) x (o) x (p)	£ _____ (q),	
Enter learning curve duration (days)	_____ (r),	
Enter non-productive % of learning curve	_____ % (s),	
Multiply (c) x (e) x [(r)/5] x (s)	£ _____ (t),	
Add (q) + (t)	£ _____ (u)	= Non-productive costs
Multiply (k) x [(c)/5] x (e)	£ _____ (v)	= Salary savings
Add (n) + (u) − (v)	£ _____ (w)	= *Replacement cost p.a.*

Potential cost saving

Enter reduced wastage rate	_____ % (aa),	
Subtract [(g) x (aa)]/(e) from (g)	£ _____ (bb),	
Subtract [(w) x (aa)]/(e) from (w)	£ _____ (cc),	
Enter current average LOS (months)	_____ (dd),	
Enter new target average LOS (months)	_____ (ee),	
Multiply [(ee)/(dd)−1] x [(g)+(w)]	£ _____ (ff),	
Expected vacancy reduction (days)	_____ (gg),	
Multiply [(n) − (v)] x [(gg)/(k)]	£ _____ (hh),	
Expected training reduction (days)	_____ (ii),	
Multiply (q) x [(ii)/(o)]	£ _____ (jj),	
Expected learning curve reduction (days)	_____ (kk),	
Multiply (t) x [(kk)/(r)]	£ _____ (ll),	
Add (bb) + (cc) + (ff) + (hh) + (jj) + (ll)	£ _____ (mm)	= *Total savings p.a.*

collect uses consistent definitions, since it is the changes over time in which you are most interested. The simplest calculation for wastage rates (or attrition or separation rates, as they are also sometimes known) is to divide the number of leavers in a given period, usually a year, by the total headcount for that same group in the period. An alternative, which reveals the extent to which an experienced workforce is being retained, is to divide the number of staff with an LOS greater than (say) 1 year by the equivalent number of staff in the same category a year ago. This provides an index of changing stability. Another commonly used check is known as cohort analysis, which looks at groups of similar employees who entered the organisation at the same time (e.g. craft apprentices or graduate trainees). This can show up specific factors, such as induction training, that may affect a whole department or team.

A good reason to make sure that you have sufficient historical data to study the trends is to identify major exceptions that happen from time to time. It is not uncommon when there is low or static wastage for a reaction to set in within a team. As the pressure builds the team initially welds itself together, but as soon as one employee flies the nest the bonds are broken for the rest – who often leave so fast that it appears to be a group decision. Although it is often unpopular, it can be better to break up such teams before they have reached that particular stage of interdependence.

One final suggestion, even if you don't carry out formal manpower modelling, is to consider the costs of a lack of *succession plans*. All the previous examples have assumed that each employee is largely interchangeable with a similarly qualified alternative – whether already on the staff or recruited from outside. If the position is supervisory or managerial, then the real cost of a mismanaged (or leaderless) department, whilst a successor learns the ropes, is likely to far outweigh any additional costs incurred via the overhead of planned succession. If the position has direct revenue responsibilities, every day the job is vacant may be costing around an additional 50% of the projected revenues.

Chapter 7

Selection and Assessment

Even if you have already deduced why labour turnover is higher in certain sections of your organisation, you still need to identify and address the various causes. Some options, such as competitive pay scales, may be difficult to tackle for current staff – at least in a single step. However, effective hiring can substantially reduce the cost of the problem in both the short and the long term.

It is taken for granted that every organisation assesses the potential suitability of external (or internal) candidates by one means or another. Unfortunately, assessment methodologies and criteria are often neither consistent not particularly effective. There are no scientific methods that guarantee success, but there are basic guidelines that should increase the likelihood that you are recruiting the right people:

- you should have a quantified reason relating to a business plan before starting any recruitment (replacement or additional)
- the requirement should be translated into a job description that states the specific outputs expected from an incumbent
- a profile of the desired candidate should then be created, with both mandatory and desirable factors noted and weighted
- depending on the selection process(es) to be used, instructions should be drawn up for consistently measuring candidates against the profile.

Many of these obvious stages are frequently skimped or even left out altogether in most organisations, usually due to the pressure of more urgent problems – which may have stemmed from earlier ineffective (or non-existent) recruitment. But far worse is when lip-service is paid to them and a 'similar' but old job description is used, giving a misleading basis for the later stages of the recruitment process.

The first point at which interpretation is likely to become wholly subjective is in defining a desirable candidate profile. It is amazing how many organisations are prepared to rely solely on interviews, particularly when the criteria used for a job are as vague as 'flexible, goal-oriented, with excellent interpersonal skills'. In an ideal world, real consistency will be derived from a detailed analysis of skills and competences in each organisation. However, much of the benefit can be gained through the less formal approach of simply allowing the profile to be drafted by the appropriate team leader on each occasion. They may need assistance but will still know better than anyone else the current team dynamics, as well as the best indicators of success and failure.

Whilst the clarity of the candidate profile (and its relevance to the job description) will have the greatest impact on productivity in the long run, it is on the short term that people most often focus. As a result, measures that relate entirely to the selection stage itself probably receive more attention than is warranted. Before starting on these, therefore, it is well to have a feel for the overall recruitment activity level and whether it is changing over time.

Hire Rates

The Accession Rate (ACR) is the ratio that gives a picture of the total amount of hiring activity in the organisation. It is a very basic indicator, calculated by dividing the number of hires in a given period by the total FTE headcount for the same period:

$$ACR = \frac{Hires}{FTE}.$$

The Replacement Rate (RER) and *the Addition Rate* (ADR) simply segment the ACR by looking separately at those hires that are refilling existing positions and those that are for new posts:

$$RER = \frac{Refills}{FTE} \quad and \quad ADR = \frac{Additions}{FTE}.$$

RER, therefore, provides one indication of the effect of labour turnover, whilst ADR shows the growth in new positions but not necessarily the overall growth since vacant jobs and redundancies have not been subtracted.

Yet it must be stressed again that there are no good or bad scores. However, the rate of change may well indicate whether the problem is a high priority or whether it can be ignored for now. For instance, if your labour turnover rate is 20% and your ACR is also 20% you might think that the two are one and the same; but your RER may be 5% and your ADR 15%. If so, then either your organisation is experiencing a major and planned reorientation in its structure or you certainly have a problem. (This can be determined by whether your current vacancies number closer to 0 or 75, on a total FTE of 500.)

As mentioned above, when people measure recruitment effectiveness, it is the short-term factors that tend to be adopted – partly, no doubt, because they can be more easily applied to each project, or even each recruiter, as performance indicators. Whilst there are dangers in applying these too literally, over time they can provide a useful means of comparison between rival agencies which are not usually responsible for the other stages in the whole process.

Every organisation will choose its own form of measures, but the majority can be grouped into four main types:

a) the time taken to fill each job
b) the time taken to hire for each job
c) the ratio of acceptances to offers
d) the direct costs for each hire.

The first of these, *Time to Fill* (TTF), is calculated by dividing the total number of days taken (from recruitment authorisation to gaining an acceptance) to fill a group of vacancies by the number of acceptances:

$$\text{TTF} = \frac{\text{days to accept}}{\text{acceptances}} .$$

In a similar vein, *Time to Hire* (TTH) takes the longer period from recruitment authorisation to actual start date and uses this in an otherwise identical calculation:

$$\text{TTH} = \frac{\text{days to hire}}{\text{acceptances}} .$$

TTF is a better measure of the effectiveness of an agency, since it is mainly dependent on their ability to provide suitable candidates at short notice. However, TTH is more relevant when identifying the scale of indirect costs impacting on the organisation.

Both ratios can be calculated for different sub-groups by location, grade or division and provide a useful base for planning when to start the recruitment project. Given the massive indirect costs incurred during recruitment, TTH also provides an indication as to where modifying the current approach would be most likely to result in cost savings.

It is probably true, however, that the average cost of hiring will be the primary measure used by the rest of the organisation and will be the most frequent cause of complaint, other than rejected job offers. Measuring these two factors should, therefore, be your concern.

The ratio of *Acceptances to Offers* (ATO) is simply calculated by dividing the number of acceptances received for a particular group of vacancies by the number of offers that had to be issued:

$$ATO = \frac{acceptances}{offers}.$$

The result will always be a figure between 0 and 1, and the aim is to get as close as possible to 1. Anything worse than 0.5 should generally suggest the need for a closer examination, since in many areas (e.g. line manager time, candidate expenses, etc) resources and costs can easily be doubled without achieving any benefit in return.

The total cost of replacing staff has already been looked at in previous chapters, but the direct costs of hiring are substantial enough. They fall into three broad groups: locating candidates, interviewing them and actually hiring them. The first contains agency/search fees and/or advertising plus any referral schemes, whilst the second group takes in interviewee expenses and the third might include relocation or buying out a contract.

The *Cost of Hires* (COH) is the total of all such costs (so long as the list remains unchanged) for a group of successful hires divided by the number of hires:

$$COH = \frac{direct\ costs}{hires}.$$

It is important to note that if you wish to include the cost of recruiters, you must be very clear as to whether you are basing these on remuneration and benefits only or on total employment costs including associated overheads. It is getting more common for some Personnel departments to re-charge, but many forget that offices and other facilities are not free and should be included in any attempt to provide a 'profitable' service.

In themselves each of these are simple ratios, but you can create your own combination as a means of putting a direct cost (and hence a value) on the recruitment process in your organisation – irrespective of whether the position is new or being refilled. You can then look at the difference between the TTH and the length of notice typically worked by a group of employees, which may indicate the level and cost of cover needed to maintain full production.

Costing recruitment effectiveness

Many organisations now realise that managing labour turnover is only one aspect of reducing the cost of employee replacement; recruitment effectiveness can have even greater impact. On average up to 60% of a Personnel department's time is spent on the clerical administration of recruitment and they typically authorise advertising and agency budgets equal to a further 2% of the total paybill. In an organisation of 500 employees, with an average wage cost of £250 per week, these costs alone will exceed *£150,000 p.a.*, before making any allowance for applicant expenses, relocation or other ancilliary items.

In addition, any delay in time to hire will require extra expenditure on cover (or will result in lost production). And, finally, incorrect selection, leading to the hiring of over- or underqualified staff, will shorten the time to next replacement, incurring further lost production followed by re-recruitment fees. The cost of this lack of quality in the selection process, for the example organisation used, could easily exceed *£300,000*.

These additional costs are generated by:

- the length of time that vacancies remain unfilled
- the investment in time and training necessary for new staff to become fully productive
- the earlier than planned repetition of the recruitment process, through the need for replacement.

And this is without accounting for any increase in absenteeism or labour turnover, due to lower morale. A computerised recruitment system which can help match profiles, as well as increase responsiveness to both applicants and line managers, should decrease the average time taken to hire. The increased quality of new hires should also lead to higher productivity, lower initial training costs and greater length of service. Taken together, these would result in direct savings of over £60,000 for our sample organisation.

BASE ASSUMPTIONS used in the above calculations are:

Number of full-time employees	= 500
Average weekly wage	= £250
Average labour turnover rate	= 10%
Average number of recruits staying < 1 year	= 20%
Average recruitment costs/fees	= 12.5% salary p.a.
Personnel staff total costs p.a.	= £60,000

Personnel time spent on recruitment   = 60%
Current time for unfilled vacancies   = 25 days
Temporary staff/overtime rates   = 1.5 × wage-rate
Current skills training per starter   = 20 days
Average cost of skills training   = £60 per day
Current learning curve duration   = 60 days
Average learning curve non-productivity   = 50%
Planned average length of service   = 60 months
Current average length of service   = 48 months
Reduced time for unfilled vacancies   = 5 days
Reduced skills training per starter   = 5 days
Reduced learning curve duration   = 15 days
Increased average length of service   = 6 months

Such figures can then be used as a basis for calculations (see p. 58), although they can also be modified to suit your specific organisation.

This approach not only indicates the scale of overall potential savings, but can suggest the processes capable of the most immediate savings. In the example described, reducing the average duration of vacancies only contributes just over 12% of the potential savings. This may be because the current duration is already quite respectable, but in any case it should encourage you to look at other aspects of the recruitment process first. If TTF is not the critical factor, then more effort can be spent on improving the quality of selection. A better fit between applicants and job requirements should contribute immediate savings of about two thirds of the potential available – and probably assist in increasing the length of service as well.

All this is important enough when you have a relatively unchanging organisation structure. If, however, you are experiencing (or are about to experience) radical change, then quality assessment and selection become even more critical – particularly if you have effective manpower and succession plans.

Sample Form for Calculation

Costing Employee Replacement

Enter number of employees	_____ (a),
Enter average weekly wage	£_____ (b),
Multiply (a) x (b)	£_____ (c),
Multiply (c) x 52	£_____ (d) = *Total paybill*
Enter current turnover rate	____%_ (e),
Enter new recruits staying < 1 year	____%_ (f),
Enter average recruitment fees	____%_ (g),
Multiply (d) x (e) x [100+(f)]/100 x (g)	£_____ (h),
Enter annual personnel staff costs	£_____ (i),
Enter % time spent on recruitment	____%_ (j),
Multiply (i) x (j) and add (h)	£_____ (k) = *Administrative costs*
Enter average vacancy duration (days)	_____ (m),
Multiplier rate for overtime/temps	_____ (n),
Multiply (b) x (n)	£_____ (o),
Multiply (a) x (e) x [100+(f)]/100 x	
(m) x [(o)/5]	£_____ (p) = *Unfilled Vacancy costs*
Enter skills training/starter (days)	_____ (q),
Enter daily cost of skills training	£_____ (r),
Multiply (a) x (e) x [100+(f)]/100 x (q) x (r)	£_____ (s),
Enter learning curve duration (days)	_____ (t),
Enter non-productive % of learning curve	____%_ (u),
Multiply (c) x (e) x [100+(f)]/100 x	
[(t)/5] x (u)	£_____ (v),
Add (s) + (v)	£_____ (w) = *Non-productive costs*
Enter planned average LOS (months)	_____ (x),
Enter actual average LOS (months)	_____ (y),
Multiply [(x)/(y)−1] x [(k)+(p)+(w)]	£_____ (z) = *Additional Repeat costs*
Multiply (m) x [(c)/5] x (e) x	
[100+(f)]/100	£_____ (A) = *Salary savings*
Add (p) + (w) + (z) − (A)	£_____ (B) = *Replacement cost p.a.*

Potential cost saving

Expected vacancy reduction (days)	_____ (1),
Multiply [(p) − (A)] x [(1)/(m)]	£_____ (2),
Expected training reduction (days)	_____ (3),
Multiply (s) x [(3)/(q)]	£_____ (4),
Expected learning curve reduction (days)	_____ (5),
Multiply (v) x [(5)/(t)]	£_____ (6),
Added actual average LOS (months)	_____ (7),
Multiply (z) x [(7)/(y)]	£_____ (8),
Add (2) + (4) + (6) + (8)	£_____ (9) = *Total Savings p.a.*

Chapter 8

Training and Re-skilling

The mismatch of skills to jobs is an additional overhead that no-one can truly afford, whether the result is individual non-performance or inefficiency in the organisational structure. One prime solution is training. Yet analysis of exit interviews has often shown that a greater demotivator than not receiving any is being given inappropriate training. Badly planned and administered training can actually lead to absenteeism and unnecessary turnover, topics which have been covered in previous chapters. Getting it right is a key to corporate success.

Despite almost universal recognition that training is essential for increased productivity and staff retention, we are also widely criticised in the UK for our lack of investment in it. There is, of course, no doubt that it is an expensive activity, both directly and in time spent outside of production, and that there has always been limited support from central government. It is, therefore, imperative that training is purchased efficiently and made available to the right people at the right time, in order to ensure minimum waste.

At present few UK organisations allocate as much as 2% of their annual paybill budget to training and development, whereas many of our European competitors frequently spend around 10%. But even if the prime objective is not automatically to reduce costs, there are few organisations that could not increase the productivity generated from their current training expenditure. Some key areas for cost control include:

- reducing wastage due to late cancellations
- negotiation over suppliers' prices and payment terms
- prioritising training in line with corporate objectives.

None of this is related to measuring the *effectiveness* of training, an exercise that many attempt only when there is pressure to slash costs or to justify the continuance of the function. Whilst it can be a fascinating project, if you have the time, most assessments are by definition very subjective. If a successful course is followed by an increase in revenues, what proportion (if any) can be directly attri-

59

buted with confidence to the training received? And of that amount how much was dependent on the specific skills imparted, as opposed to the improvement in knock-on factors (motivation, peer recognition, the break from routine)?

According to the Training Agency, fewer than 20% of UK organisations in 1987 made any attempt to review the benefits of training against the costs incurred. Whatever the truth of this claim, there is no excuse for not controlling basic costs. For example, do you know the total training requirements for new and promoted staff? Relevant information from efficient administration would allow you to negotiate far better with suppliers and can even increase your chances when applying for Government grants.

The most important aspect is to have an audit of currently available skills and those required to undertake the jobs. The latter should be derived by cascading down from corporate business and HR plans to objective-setting and individual appraisals. A computerised system, providing an accurate needs analysis, will help achieve scheduling of course programmes. When combined with budget control, this can easily reduce costs by at least 15% – or, more sensibly, allow an increase of 17.5% in the amount of extra training delivered for no extra cost. (Yes, a reduction of wastage by 15% will allow you to deliver an extra 17.5% within your original budget: a budget of £100 with wastage of £15 is only delivering £85 worth, so increasing delivery to £100 is an increase of just over 17.5% [(100/85 × 100) − 100].)

In a typical organisation, used as an example throughout this book, the training budget would be of the order of £130,000 – and the amount of money thereby freed up for re-use would be £19,500 p.a. (or more if a Government grant is now obtained). This takes no account of any indirect costs or savings.

BASE ASSUMPTIONS used in the above calculations are:

Number of full-time employees	= 500
Number of working days p.a.	= 235
Average weekly wage	= £250
Training/development budget	= 2% of paybill budget
Current course cancellations	= 10% of bookings
Courses booked for private needs	= 10% of bookings
Improvement in suppliers' terms	= 10%
Reduction in course cancellations	= 25%
Reduction in unnecessary courses	= 25%
Total grant/subsidy gained	= £15,000

The 'Courses booked for private needs' refer to courses booked at the direct behest of individuals without a formal analysis of what they need to do their job. On these assumptions we can build a simple framework for calculating the scale of the particular opportunity for your organisation, including any additional grant obtained.

Sample Form for Calculation

Costing training and development

Enter number of employees	_____ (a),	
Enter average weekly wage	£ _____ (b),	
Multiply (a) x (b)	£ _____ (c),	
Multiply (c) x 52	£ _____ (d)	= Total paybill
Enter % of paybill for training	_____ % (e),	
Multiply (d) x (e)	£ _____ (f)	= Training budget
Enter % of courses cancelled	_____ % (g),	
Enter courses for individual needs	_____ % (h),	
Add (g) + (h)	_____ % (i),	
Multiply (f) x (i)	£ _____ (j)	= Cost of potential waste

Maximising training and development

Improvement in suppliers' terms	_____ % (k),	
Reduction in course cancellations	_____ % (l),	
Reduction in unnecessary courses	_____ % (m),	
Multiply (f) x (k)	£ _____ (n),	
Multiply (f) x (g) x (l)	£ _____ (o),	
Multiply (f) x (h) x (m)	£ _____ (p),	
Enter total grant/subsidy gained	£ _____ (q),	
Add (n) + (o) + (p) + (q)	£ _____ (r)	= Total savings p.a.

Whilst items (k) and (l) are presumed to be self-explanatory, item (m) is likely to be less immediately obvious. Where item (h) is the percentage of all courses that were previously booked on the unplanned basis of individual demand, (m) is the percentage of them that are no longer deemed necessary once needs analysis creates a better focus on relevant courses.

However, training is fairly unusual amongst HR activities in having a visible cost directly associated with it and yet also being predictable and recurrent, much like pay. (It may be these factors that have caused some organisations to consider the provision of training as an element of remuneration, leading to conflict as to what proportion constitutes a prepayment recoverable if termination predates the shelf-life of the training.) This whole principle of apportioning costs to the period over which a return on investment is achieved has even caused sharp words between subsidiaries or in companies with multi-national sites. To put it simply, managers object to paying for the training of an individual without receiving the full benefit themselves.

It may, therefore, be helpful also to look at some measurements that provide a quick indication of changes in the cost and quantity of training being delivered. Once again, this requires consistency in the definitions used:

Training costs (TC) = the total costs associated with training during the period, including the expenses of the Training department and any direct costs – whoever actually pays for them.

Training hours (TH) = the duration in hours of a course multiplied by the number of attendees, totalled up for all courses during the period.

Trained numbers (TN) = the number of employees who received any training during the period.

Simple ratios can be derived from these values and then monitored over time to determine trends and the rate of actual change, whether this was planned or not. Whilst anyone can create their own ratios, some suggestions include:

The average cost of training all employees:

$$\frac{TC}{HC}.$$

A similar effect can be achieved by splitting TC into the sub-totals of individual courses or course types and then repeating the calculation shown.

A simple indicator of the average amount of training provided to employees, based on the number of hours delivered, is:

$$\frac{TH}{HC}.$$

An alternative to this is a similar indicator using only those employees who have received some training:

$$\frac{TH}{TN}.$$

A comparison between these two ratios may show an untenable imbalance in the delivery of training. Further investigation can be carried out by looking at the percentage of employees that received any training during the period:

$$\frac{TN}{HC}.$$

When compared, these ratios can give a clearer picture of the distribution of training throughout the organisation, or within a division, as shown in Figure 16.

	Sales A	Sales B	Sales C	All Sales	Company
Training per head (£s)	365	682	260	429	260
Training per head (hrs)	11.7	21.8	8.3	13.7	5.2
Percentage of employees receiving training	91.7	90.9	91.7	91.4	38.6
Training per employee trained (£s)	398	750	284	469	674
Training per employee trained (hrs)	12.7	24.0	9.1	15.0	13.5

Notes: More hours and £s were spent on training Sales people than the company average, but this is accounted for by Team B.
Teams A and C received less training than the company average.

Figure 16   Analysis of Training Delivered

Finally, even if you are now managing to deliver more training within your budget and can justify the distribution of training activity, there still remains the question of measuring the *impact* of the courses. Without a proper plan based on needs analysis, it is common to find some of the following problems:

• training delivered but only partially (or not at all) used, due to incorrect timing or mismatch of requirements

- training delivered too late, causing unnecessary inefficiency in current job
- training delivered by rota, with no clearly defined purpose or objective.

Whilst assessing whether or not a course has delivered the needs of the individual (or department) must remain subjective, expectations and satisfaction can be measured. To a lesser extent, performance changes can also sometimes be measured, if benchmarks are established in advance – although there will always be room for dispute as to the degree of cause and effect. The correct interpretation of such figures is as much a job for psychologists as for statisticians and other mere mortals, so it will not be attempted here. Nevertheless, it is certainly worth making the measurements, particularly if professional guidance is sought in setting the system up correctly.

So far in this chapter the emphasis has been on practical management of the training budget. The impact of general skills shortages can be even more profound in the case of new staff and/or organisational restructuring. Slightly less scientific, but still of some practical use, are two other aspects of training which can be costed:

- a reduction in the learning curve (non-productive time)
- a reduction in scrap-rates, through increased performance and output quality.

For instance, training costs could be defined as the payroll costs of trainers and delegates, the costs of course materials and facilities, general administration and the 'opportunity' cost of having allocated employees to a course rather than leaving them on productive work. You might believe, or even have quasi-scientific proof, that certain training courses in new technology dramatically reduce the learning curve – from an average 50% productivity level for three months to an average 50% for only the first two months. If the weekly output target has a sales value of £8,000 per production worker, then training each of them when they start might cost the organisation £9,290 per head but generate additional revenues in the next three months of £20,000 (see Figure 17a).

Alternatively, you might be more interested in the effect of training on the *quality* of output – as measured by scrap-rates. For instance, it might be possible to determine that the scrap-rates drop from 5% to 3% immediately after training, rather than after 3 months' hands-on experience (see Figure 17b). This might deliver savings of £208 per head. If the relevant workforce is 50 strong with 20% turnover, then the introduction of a formal one-week induction training course held quarterly might cost £92,900 p.a. but show savings of £202,080 p.a. – easily justifying the investment.

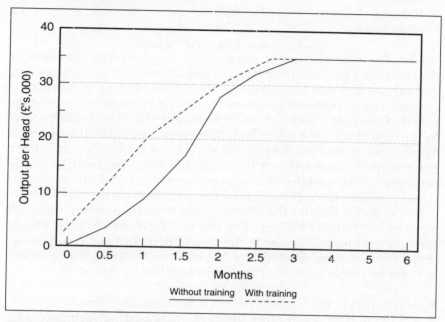

Figure 17a   Impact of Training on Output

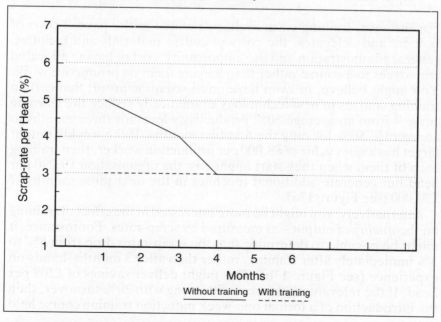

Figure 17b   Impact of Training on Scrap-rates

Chapter 9

Remuneration and Benefits

Remuneration is undoubtedly the most visible of all costs associated with HR, yet it is the least understood and controlled element. This is usually due to the fragmented way in which every part of the organisation demands a say in it, whilst none is prepared to accept ultimate accountability for its control.

Individuals know how much more (never less) they should be earning, managers have views on who are more deserving than others, Finance wants the total increase kept as close to 0% as possible and may in certain circumstances/areas want a reduction, and Personnel is caught in the middle trying to deliver a structure that will appeal to all these parties. Like all compromises based on conflicting demands, the only certainty is that none will be met in their entirety. This is hardly a recipe for truly winning hearts and minds, which is why there is almost always a degree of drift in costs.

At this point the beginning of a vicious circle may become apparent. More than one Finance Director has decided that if drift is a relatively constant factor then it should be built into the total cost assumptions. Since, however, it is not part of what is 'on offer', the apparently available budget is reduced. The gap between demands and budgets is thereby widened and the likelihood of anyone being satisfied is reduced still further. The missing ingredient is trust – by Finance that expenditure will be maintained within budgets and by employees that they are getting a fair share of the rewards.

The temptation is to make promises to all parties and then try to manage your way through any mishaps in implementation. This is certain to lead to a lose-lose situation, since any lack in clarity will always be interpreted by each party to their advantage – leading you back to where you started, a conflict of expectations.

If, however, you can gain the trust of the Finance department, by demonstrating an appreciation of their concerns and by reducing any unplanned drift in costs, you will be able to concentrate on the expectations of managers. This in turn can help reduce the gap between the demands of individuals and what they receive. In other words, don't compromise but tackle each area in turn and start with Finance, since this will define the scope of what you can offer.

Gaining the confidence of the Finance department requires involvement at the planning stage, information during the administration and demonstrable savings afterwards.

Before even commencing any negotiation or review processes, accurate costing is a fundamental part of planned reward management. It is also a prerequisite for communicating to staff, in understandable terms, the real value of benefits. These are often wrongly regarded as the flexible element in remuneration. It is very easy to increase their cost, but several studies have shown that they quickly become base 'norms' and lose any intended motivational value. Since they are virtually impossible to reduce later, their controlled use is paramount and needs to be carefully costed and planned.

This is not the place to enter into the complexities of designing a remuneration package, but it is worth remembering the wide range of elements that may be under consideration. Over and above legislative demands (tax rates, national insurance rates, SSP and SMP), there are various types of pay (direct, bonus, profit-related), all with their own regulations depending on specific criteria. But the widest net is cast by basic and fringe benefits, from the almost ubiquitous (pensions, expenses, company cars) to industry- or organisation-specific items (cheap mortgages, use of company-owned assets, products manufactured by the company). All this is not to forget assistance with relocation, private health and education or overseas cost-of-living adjustments. And then there are the latest tax office judgements on topics as diverse as employee share schemes, cash alternatives to company cars and subsidised canteens.

Even without a formalised cafeteria system of benefits from which employees can make an individual choice, it is surprising how few organisations can list all the benefits they provide and the costs associated with each one, let alone the actual take-up in the course of the financial year. Whilst it may be impossible to quantify accurately in advance the cost of introducing a new benefit such as paternity leave, this is no excuse for not attempting a basic forecast. If your organisation is large enough, then a brief study of the previous year's absences (and the reasons recorded for them) may give you useful data. Alternatively, you could use Government (CSO) statistics or, if your organisation is sufficiently small, personal knowledge to hazard a reasonable estimate. Unless this exercise is carried out, however, the benefit is being given without management appreciating the likely cost or employees appreciating the value.

Some Useful Ratios

As a simple way of identifying whether your organisation is suffering from a creeping increase in the cost of benefits, you can calculate some basic ratios. The definitions used in Chapter 1 can be re-applied. In each case, it is the change in the ratio over time that you will want to note, not any absolute value.

Benefits over Revenues (BOR) is derived by dividing the total costs of your benefits programme by the total operating revenues for the same period (usually monthly or quarterly):

$$BOR = \frac{BE}{RE}.$$

In this way you can monitor the relative increase in costs to revenues as one likely indicator of changes in profitability.

The Benefits Expenses Ratio (BER), by contrast, is used when you are more interested in the percentage of total operational expenses represented by the cost of the benefits programme. It is calculated by dividing the cost of benefits by total expenses and then multiplying by 100:

$$BER = \frac{BE \times 100}{EX}.$$

Benefits per Profit (BPP) is a particularly appropriate ratio when the majority of your benefits programme is intended to be directly allied to profits generated over a specified time. It is generated by dividing the cost of benefits by gross profit for the same period:

$$BPP = \frac{BE}{PR}.$$

As you gather more detailed data on the individual benefits, it may be worth devising your own ratios – showing, for instance, the percentage of total benefit represented by one or more particular benefits. As with a share portfolio, it is generally recommended that you spread the risk by not allowing any one benefit to become dominant in the total mix.

Did you know that the benefits element in remuneration packages, as published cases have shown, can double the total value? But although the benefits package is an expensive and increasingly complex part of total remuneration, the control of basic salaries or wages remains paramount. Do you know the true cost of total employee and staff remuneration month by month? Could you model alternative schemes at salary review time and cost them?

Since it is still true that few organisations can with confidence even give an accurate figure for their headcount, it is perhaps not too surprising that they rarely know what each position is really worth – on the open market or to the organisation. Consequently, individual employees are often overpaid or underpaid in apparently random fashion. The result, if outside opportunities exist, will often be that competent but underpaid employees do not stay with you while overpaid employees remain.

In addition to researching valid data for local market rates, it is essential to have an effective salary and grade structure that allows proper comparison of positions within your organisation and industry when it is time for any planning. Actually bringing wage rates into line with the market is not easy and may involve red-circling some positions or even proactive replacement of the incumbent. But, if correctly targeted, it is likely to increase overall productivity and other performance measures. Although official statistics do not exist, individual organisations introducing clear structures have reported direct savings of at least 3–5% on the paybill in the first year alone.

As stated earlier, however, it is just as important to keep the Finance department in the picture during *administration* of the paybill as it was during planning of the salary review. The aim should be to move away from a reliance on the annual exercise of budget setting (that is only monitored historically) to a dynamic on-going process.

Pay Drift

This is where controlling, or at least reducing, drift comes into play. It is not uncommon, irrespective of recession or economic boom, for organisations to experience pay drift of up to 10% p.a. Many are simply unaware of the problem, whilst others cannot find the right control mechanisms. At first sight, this may not seem like much of a problem; after all, you manage despite this every year. Yet, translated into equivalent headcount, a company with 500 staff and steady 10% wage drift is paying for 25 phantom staff over budget plan without making any comparable contribution to profits.

Drift can occur in many, often unacknowledged, ways, including:

earnings drift generated by unplanned overtime, piece-rate and bonus payments *grade drift* resulting from organisational restructuring (pseudo-promotions) and group (comparability) agreements

salary drift, when merit/profit/commission payments become wholly or partially consolidated into salaries

replacement drift, when rates are adjusted (always upwards) after new staff are hired – sometimes for more than the rate refused to the person who therefore resigned

benefits drift, where the controlling policy is not enforced through lack of clarity or monitoring.

It is not easy to acquire all the myriad items of data that together would allow you to quantify the relative scale of the problem in your organisation. Almost certainly you will need a computerised system, with salary and grade structures, showing a proper comparison of jobs and generating reports that identify trends and exceptions. When used for modelling, negotiation and market rate comparisons it can typically result in at least a 25% reduction in the total drift. Since most organisations now find that the full range of benefits add 30% or more to the paybill, the potential realistic savings from controlling drift are of the order of 3–5% p.a. of the paybill.

Costing Total Pay Drift

In the organisation used as an example in earlier chapters, the cost of total drift could easily be £845,000 p.a. on top of the annual paybill of £6.5m – of which at least £260,000 could be saved through clearer communication and monitoring.

BASE ASSUMPTIONS used in the above calculations are:

Number of full-time employees	= 500
Average weekly wage	= £250
Current total pay drift	= 10%
Reduction in total pay drift	= 25%
Additional cost of benefits	= 30% of paybill
Current total benefits drift	= 10%
Reduction in total benefits drift	= 50%

Although a very simple model, which you will no doubt wish to amend and then add to, the example given has the merit of being easy to complete. If this shows the cost-saving potential to be substantial, then it will be worthwhile spending time on developing your own model.

Sample Form for Calculation

Costing total pay drift

Enter number of employees	————	(a),
Enter average weekly wage	£————	(b),
Multiply (a) x (b) x 52	£————	(c) = Total paybill
Enter average drift of earnings	————%	(d),
Enter average drift of grades	————%	(e),
Enter average drift of salaries	————%	(f),
Add (d) + (e) + (f)	————%	(g) = Total pay drift
Multiply (a) x (g)	————	(h) = 'Additional' staff
Multiply (c) x (g)	£————	(i) = Pay drift cost p.a.
Enter total pensions contribution	£————	(j),
Enter total health scheme costs	£————	(k),
Enter total life-assurance cost	£————	(l),
Enter total allowances/expenses	£————	(m),
Enter total costs of company cars	£————	(n),
Enter other discretionary costs	£————	(o),
Add (j)+(k)+(l)+(m)+(n)+(o)	£————	(p) = Total benefits bill
Multiply [(p)/(c)] x 100	————%	(q) = Paybill addition due to benefits
Enter average drift of benefits	————%	(r),
Multiply (p) x (r)	£————	(s) = Benefits drift cost p.a.
Add (i) + (s)	£————	(t) = Remuneration drift p.a.

Potential cost saving

Expected reduction in pay drift	————%	(u),
Multiply (i) x (u)	£————	(v) = Pay drift savings
Expected reduction in benefits drift	————%	(w),
Multiply (s) x (w)	£————	(x) = Benefits drift savings
Add (v) + (x)	£————	(y) = Total savings p.a.

Care must be taken with percentages, particularly where one is being applied to another percentage figure. For instance, items (g) and (r) are the drift percentages of total pay and benefits respectively; whereas items (u) and (w) are percentages of items (g) and (r) respectively.

Attention in this chapter has been focussed almost entirely on measuring the true cost of compensation and benefits packages and on reducing the drift element. This is not to say that other financial measures should not be in place. Indeed, several have been mentioned in passing, such as salary planning and budgeting procedures and competitive positioning via salary surveys. But these are usually better understood already so a note of caution rather than detailed exposition is probably appropriate here. Paying too little attention to the local sensitivities of surveys to apparent minutiae often causes greater problems than ignoring them altogether. Unless your organisation is sufficiently large and structured to be able to identify clear comparators, joining (or setting up) a local employers' salary club is likely to be more productive.

Ultimately, the strategic framework of remuneration packages should be designed to reinforce the desired culture. Confusing this with a concerted rush to performance-related pay recently caused much grief in organisations, where even the luckiest have often spent money unnecessarily without either motivating staff or increasing profitability. Connections between pay and incentives, productivity and reward, are extremely complex and do not lend themselves to general models. Nevertheless, some aspects of rewarding success can be measured, and the results tracked over time for comparison with the costs incurred.

Chapter 10

The Flexible Workforce

The recently discovered need for a flexible approach when determining employment terms for staff seems to be remarkably resilient to changing economic and demographic factors. At one stage it was driven by the need to attract more people into the labour market; now it is more often seen as a way of minimising fixed costs. Indeed the specific reasons given by organisations are extremely varied.

Perhaps the reason for this is that the underlying objective is unaffected by outside factors. At long last, organisations are shifting their focus from 'getting the most out of our resources' to defining the resources needed to best deliver the required outputs. This subtle but important distinction is analogous to the problem I have seen set in a management development programme: 'You cross a bridge and, while walking along the riverbank, you see someone in distress. You grab one of the three lifebelts available and throw it in. You are about to go for help when another person floats by. As you reach for another lifebelt, two more people appear in the water upstream. What would you do?'

The lateral suggestion is to go upstream and find out who or what is throwing the people off the bridge in the first place. Tackling the cause rather than the symptoms may sound obvious, but the majority of respondents opt for trying to save those visibly in distress – an impossibility on your own, particularly if the numbers continue to increase further. In a similar fashion, many organisations find that their HR plans are trying to maximise productivity of the general workforce without refining the underlying structure and working patterns to suit the required outputs.

A standard job is often thought of as having regular hours and being based at a fixed location (office/factory/shop). A single person, who expects a continuous career with some degree of progression, is employed to fill each post until they leave or are promoted. Each of these expectations is challenged by at least one type of flexible working:

- flexible hours (from flexitime to annual-hours contracts)
- job sharing (more than one person per job and sometimes vice versa)

73

- career breaks (for family, educational or other personal reasons)
- tele-commuting (whether home-based or permanently mobile)
- international secondment for fixed-term projects.

Although there can be considerable overlap between each area, they are worth looking at individually without attempting to value their combined potential benefit to the organisation.

Flexible Hours

Flexitime has been around in some industries for a long time and only varies from the standard job, described previously, in one respect. Each individual is free to determine the hours that they work each day, within certain specified constraints such as time ranges within which work must be started and finished each day, and a minimum number of days per month that must be worked.

The fewer the constraints, the more interdependencies between jobs become unreliable, so the rules will usually be adapted to particular types of work rather than applied across the whole organisation. The approach is almost entirely designed to bring benefit to employees, who can fit their individual work pattern to other factors (such as transportation schedules or school hours) over which they have no control. When correctly applied, however, it should not attract additional direct costs for the organisation and can generate indirect savings via reduced absenteeism or wastage, as well as increasing the pool of potential applicants. A less well publicised advantage for employers is that this can be one of the least contentious ways of introducing the recording of time sheets (electronically or otherwise).

Amongst the more extreme variations of this approach are what are usually termed annual-hours contracts. Instead of simply looking at the total number of hours per week or month to be worked, these contracts are based on a predetermined number of hours per year. They differ from flexitime in that the employer, not the employee, usually determines the application of most of these hours. This can solve any one of a number of problems that an organisation may be facing:

- cyclical/seasonal patterns of work for one or more business units
- the need for a just-in-time response to unpredictable client demand/peaks
- excessive overtime costs and/or general overmanning
- expensive plant/equipment used at a less than optimum level
- gradual expansion without large boosts in investment levels.

Although these are predominantly productivity issues, a simple example can show the kind of savings that might be directly attributed to this approach.

If your Production division employs 250 people at an average salary of £250 per week and average overtime is running at 5%, your annual paybill for the function is £3,412,500. On an annual-hours basis, if you suffer from one of the problems mentioned above, you may be able to reduce the hours needed to only 85% of those currently covered by standard hours and yet reduce overtime to a mere 2%. You could award a 13% pay-rise, as an introduction to the scheme and in compensation for loss of overtime, and still show a net saving of £228,500.

BASE ASSUMPTIONS used in the above calculations are:

Number of employees in division	= 250
Average current weekly basic wage	= £250
Current average overtime earnings per employee p.a.	= £650
Current contractual number of working-hours per week	= 37.5
Introductory/compensatory pay-rise	= 13%
New average overtime earnings per employee p.a.	= £250
New contractual number of working-hours per year	= 1657.5

You can apply data from your own organisation in a similar manner through the calculations shown on p. 76. As can be seen, the employees benefit: 98% of their annual earnings are now 'guaranteed' (rather than dependent on overtime), compared to only 95% before. In addition their basic earnings will still be 97% of the original level, despite having to work for only 85% of the hours.

The organisation benefits most visibly through substantial savings in direct employment costs, even without allowing for improvements in wastage and absenteeism that often appear to accompany this approach. By only applying the resources when they are needed, additional savings will also tend to accrue (e.g. from being able to maintain plant during the working week). Furthermore, as well as reducing unit production costs, it may now be possible to use some of the savings to fund more training and thereby further increase quality output.

Sample Form for Calculation

Costing the standard contract

Enter number of employees in division	_____ (a),	
Enter average weekly basic wage	£ _____ (b),	
Enter average overtime earnings per employee p.a.	£ _____ (c),	
Enter contractual number of working-hours per week	_____ (d),	
Add [(b) x 52] + (c)	£ _____ (e)	= Employee annual earnings
Multiply (d) x 52	_____ (f),	
Multiply (a) x (e)	£ _____ (g)	= Paybill p.a.

Costing annual hours

Enter introductory pay-rise	_____ % (h),	
Multiply [(b)/(d)] x [(h)/100] and add [(b)/(d)]	£ _____ (i),	
Enter new average overtime earnings per employee p.a.	£ _____ (j),	
Enter contractual number of working-hours per year	_____ (k),	
Add [(i) x (k)] + (j)	£ _____ (m)	= Employee annual earnings
Multiply (a) x (m)	£ _____ (n)	= Paybill p.a.
Divide [(b) x 52] by (e)	_____ % (o)	= Old guaranteed earnings rate
Divide [(i) x (k)] by (m)	_____ % (p)	= New guaranteed earnings rate
Divide [(i) x (k)] by [(b) x 52]	_____ % (q)	= Portion of old basic still received
Divide (k) by [(d) x 52]	_____ % (r)	= Portion of old hours still worked
Subtract (n) from (g)	£ _____ (s)	= Paybill saving

Job Sharing

This is another much vaunted initiative which has proved very successful in a number of cases and was one of the main planks, for several organisations, in the introduction of equal opportunity policies. Job sharing, in theory, simply means taking a single job and splitting it into two (or occasionally more) portions, which are then allocated to different people. This benefits employees who cannot (or are unwilling to) cover 'standard' hours, whilst the organisation gains access to an additional pool of talent.

Although job sharing is sometimes confused with part-time work, the important distinction is that a *whole* job is being performed – with equal status and responsibilities to similar jobs that happen to be occupied by a single individual. However, to be effective, job sharing requires a more detailed analysis of job tasks than is commonly available and their proper allocation between the partners, including arrangements for time. There is often also a need for preparation of the department or unit in which the job share will operate.

Frequent complaints from job sharers are that they feel every minute has to be fully occupied with visible work and that they have to work longer than their contractual hours just to stand still. Phrases like 'I can't stop for a coffee, I'm only here for 4 hours' and 'I'll do the reports when I get home' are heard with great regularity. This need to prove equality with full-time employees can be self-defeating, however, since it ensures that there is less time to pick up informal information.

The key to success in job sharing is effective integration, both between the partners and with the whole organisation. A clear understanding and joint ownership of the job is obviously essential if there is to be quality output. This is probably both the greatest strength and weakness of job sharing – that interdependencies are typically strongest between the partners and not with the rest of the organisation.

If the requirement is for relatively scarce skills to be applied within a function that operates fairly independently of teams, then job sharing can be extremely effective. It can also be used as a mutually beneficial way of maintaining near-continuous employment for staff who need temporarily to reduce their working hours (e.g. after the birth of a child). Indeed, there are reports that some of the most productive are the rare partnerships made up of husband and wife teams.

The down-side is that, so far, there are very few examples of job sharing being applied successfully to senior roles. There are sheer practical complexities at this level, but the primary factor is lack of acceptance by the rest of the management team. When only applied to unskilled positions, however, job sharing invariably becomes a euphemism for part-time or shift work without any of the intended benefits. Without a major shift in cultural attitudes, it seems doomed to remain an effective tool only for skilled, fairly independent people operating at not too senior a level.

Since there is still one full-time job being carried out, there are rarely major changes in cost – in either direction. The most immediate financial implications are generally negative, although not substantially so. Because there is currently a cap for salaries above which National Insurance is not levied, a single salary split into two may attract a higher total levy. A more tenuous problem that has been mentioned applies to the trend for staff to take a computer home with them to finish off reports. This is often impossible with job sharing, unless double the amount of equipment is purchased.

Productivity, however, is often higher, for the kind of reasons mentioned earlier. Absenteeism tends to be much lower for equally basic reasons (i.e. a desire not to let one's partner down and greater opportunities to fit outside activities around the job). I am not, however, aware of scientific evidence that has quantified these aspects and can only suggest that the models described earlier can be adapted in your own organisation to determine whether this approach brings identifiable financial benefits.

Career Breaks

By definition, this could be better regarded as a more flexible approach to *not* working. Yet it can be a valid tool in flexibly managing careers to the mutual benefit of employee and organisation. Most schemes are designed specifically to allow high-calibre staff with future potential to re-enter the organisation at the same grade or level of seniority after a specified period of absence.

The benefit to the organisation encompasses both goodwill and the likely return of valuable skills and knowledge that will be accompanied by a high degree of commitment. The greatest take-up is by women who would not return under the normal maternity leave provisions, but who would like to maintain a career after 2 years or so. It is equally appropriate for anyone who wishes to undertake a substantial project outside of the work environment (e.g. further studies, travel, caring for a relative, voluntary work, etc).

The most obvious cost savings are the reduction (but not complete eradication) in recruitment costs and the compressed learning curve for returners to employment. However, these have to be weighed against the additional costs of filling in for the interim period, which (if the organisation is not in a major mode of expansion and therefore able to make continuing use of the additional resource) can outweigh the quantifiable savings.

Telecommuting

Possibly even more than the other categories mentioned, this kind of flexible working attracts employees characterised by high levels of autonomy and self-regulation. This is partly because they often have a large role in negotiating the position, but also because they are unlikely to succeed without such traits.

There are many different definitions of this type of work, often referred to as 'home-working', although the spread of low-cost communications technology has led to the term 'telecommuting'. The common denominator is that the employee usually has no space retained on their behalf at the organisation's premises, but relies on their home – or, in rare cases, mobile vehicle – as a base for working and communicating with the outside world via telephones, computers with modems and/or fax machines.

Despite the presumed ecological benefits and the potential for an improved quality of family life, it is still less than 1% of the UK workforce which is actually living this way – and most of these are self-employed rather than true telecommuters. Apart from the usual reluctance to accept change, there are two primary reasons for this slow uptake. The main one is that, almost by definition, it is rarely applicable to front-office jobs where teamwork is important and where clients need to be able to locate staff easily. If these are significant aspects of the job and yet are compromised, any saving will be quickly swamped by lost productivity and/or revenues.

The other reason is that this approach can seldom be introduced for straightforward reasons of cost-justification – unless the organisation manages to slip some of the normal employment liabilities and costs onto the employee without paying compensation. For instance, the most obvious saving (the reduction in office space and associated utilities) can only be achieved if saleable chunks are released and there is a buyer to take the costs off the hands of the organisation. Frequently, the net result is simply more space for remaining staff or a vacant building for which no taker can be found. Neither of these situations reduces costs noticeably, so telecommuting is more sensibly introduced as an adjunct to other major changes – such as closing divisions or opening new facilities – when real savings can be achieved.

Additional costs, however, are often immediately visible. Many items of equipment (e.g. telephones, photocopiers, fax machines, PCs, printers, etc) that are available on a shared basis in the office may not be suitable for home use and will have to be replaced. Other capital costs will arise in ensuring that the home-base complies with basic legislation such as Health and Safety rules.

Then there are the additional employee costs due to general issues of communications, monitoring and training. These all relate to the difficulties experienced by staff who have no regular face-to-face contact with colleagues, let alone formal supervision. One particular side-effect is that they often require a greater amount of formal training, since they have less opportunity to learn from their peers on the job.

On top of all this, employees often find they are faced with unexpected hurdles and costs relating to their intended use of residential premises for work. Many mortgage lenders place strict constraints on the use to which premises may be put and local authorities have been known to interpret homes used for telecommuting as 'light industrial' for the purposes of planning permission. Insurance cover may be invalidated or need amending and, worst of all, your sole residence may suddenly lose (at least partially) exemption from Capital Gains Tax when you come to sell it.

A new variation that attempts to avoid these types of problem is the satellite office. This is a purpose-designed unit that nevertheless operates much as a home-based unit would do, but located in a local high street to which many individuals (not necessarily from one organisation) have easy access. The problem is that, unless it is *very* local, it is of no benefit to employees – who might as well commute to the proper office. Other than as a temporary fix, therefore, it tends to be like most compromises, the worst of both worlds, unattractive to employees but still incurring fixed costs for the organisation.

A more successful spin-off from this approach is where the organisation offers employees the opportunity and assistance in setting up as freelance consultants, with a certain amount of guaranteed work for the first year or two. There are so many variables at play here that it can be exceedingly complex to calculate the real benefit, but a few hints may suffice to get you started.

For the organisation, a rough rule of thumb might be that the cost of keeping someone as an employee is approximately 2.5 times their salary. This breaks down typically into three elements: the salary itself, half as much again for related benefits and taxes, and the equivalent of the salary in associated overhead facilities. As a further rough approximation, the sum being spent for a typical employee comes out at around 4 times their *net* earnings.

If the employee becomes a freelance contractor, however, and charges the organisation at a rate of two-thirds of the costs incurred as an employee, it is possible that they will both show a gain. If the organisation only needs these services for 4 months of the year, they can reduce their costs by over 77% – while the ex-employee is submitting invoices worth over 92% of previous annual earnings. Tax still has to be paid, but under a far more preferential regime than PAYE, and there is the opportunity to work for the remaining 8 months of the year on other contracts.

BASE ASSUMPTIONS used in the above calculations are:

Basic annual salary of particular employee	= £30,000
Cost of providing benefits package (car, pension, etc)	= £10,000
Cost to organisation of tax and NI	= £5,000
Apportioned cost of overheads for this employee	= £30,000
Employee tax deductions	= £8,500
Employee NI deductions	= £1,600
Employee pension contributions	= £1,500
Agreed contractor day-rate	= £200
Number of weeks p.a. to be contracted	= 17 weeks

These assumptions are round numbers. Precise figures will vary with the circumstances of the individual and would have to take account of payroll legislation. Similar calculations can be applied to data within your own organisation, if this is a relevant option to investigate, with any variations that you feel are appropriate (see p. 82). The main points are that employees are getting a low-risk opportunity to set themselves up in business, whilst the organisation retains an immediate option on valuable knowledge at substantially reduced costs.

International Secondment

All the previous options are aimed either at competing for scarce skills or reducing costs for the organisation, and in some cases both. This section is something of an anomaly, although it does share one theme with the other topics: the move towards ownership of careers by employees rather than by just the organisation.

Until fairly recently it was felt that international postings were a

---

Sample Form for Calculation

Costing direct employment

Enter employee basic annual salary   £ _____ (a),
Enter cost of providing benefits
    package   £ _____ (b),
Enter cost to organisation of tax and NI   £ _____ (c),
Enter apportioned cost of overheads
    for employee   £ _____ (d),
Add (a) + (b) + (c) + (d)   £ _____ (e) = Cost to organisation

Enter employee tax deductions   £ _____ (f),
Enter employee NI deductions   £ _____ (g),
Enter employee pension contributions   £ _____ (h),
Subtract [(f) + (g) + (h)] from (a)   £ _____ (i) = Employee annual earnings

Costing the contractor option

Enter the agreed contractor day-rate   £ _____ (j),
Enter the number of weeks to be
    contracted   _____ (k),
Multiply (j) x (k) x 5   £ _____ (m) = Cost to organisation
    and = Before-tax contractor earnings

Subtract (m) from (e)   £ _____ (n) = Savings for organisation
Subtract [100 x (m)/(e)] from 100.0   _____ % (o) = Savings for organisation
Divide [(m) x 100] by (i)   _____ % (p) = Portion of original earnings

---

career in themselves requiring special employees – often called expatriates – but this is now broadly discredited. Amongst the reasons for this change of heart is the realisation that most individuals find the impact on family life increasingly unacceptable, particularly if they become involved in a continuous process of change. It is now also recognised that local management is an essential component of any overseas operation, and that any person posted abroad must assimilate themselves into the particular culture. Few people can achieve this and fewer still can do so across multiple cultures.

Nevertheless, international postings remain a valuable part of the flexible workforce, for a different reason. As part of the training package for 'high-flyers' in truly international organisations, fixed-term overseas contracts, often with a specific objective and usually at a comparatively junior level, are an extremely valuable element of career management.

The costs can be substantial and so will usually only be considered by large organisations, either where there is a trouble-shooting role (and payback can be measured direct) or as part of management-development budgets. International benefits and remuneration are sufficiently complex for people to specialise solely in advising on them. No attempt will be made to tackle them here but, as an example, the issues may include:

• taxation and social security across multiple frontiers
• exchange rate conversion and currency purchasing
• moving expenses and cost of living/leave allowances
• salary differentials and conflicts (home-based and social).

Other special service conditions may apply to assistance with housing or even the cost of education for children. The selection process will also need to be much more rigorous than usual, even for existing employees, since the psychological fit will be very important – not just generally for international secondment but for country-specific issues. In total, these will come to a very large sum, and the main requirement will be to manage the budgets effectively rather than to achieve savings.

Most of the examples given have focussed on the flexibility of organisational policies first and the flexibility of the people second. This is partly because that reflects the purpose of this book, but no-one should underestimate the impact on the individuals involved. Without exception, they will experience a sense of total isolation from time to time and will need special support. Any organisation that sees flexibility as a cheap approach to employment and a way to avoid responsibility for staff welfare will reap poor rewards in productive output.

One of the main benefits is that all these approaches encourage a project mentality, where predetermined and measurable targets are set for fixed periods of time. This focus, in turn, instead of basing structures on when and where work is carried out, can help the move to increased awareness of quality and improved performance. Like all HR options, however, it will only work if there is an opportunity for real benefit to both the employees and the organisation.

In the future, an employee may well work for an organisation for many years in a variety of ways. They may start as a trainee before moving on to a full-time position, then take a career break followed by a period of job sharing, finally returning to a full-time post and ending in a consultancy relationship. Alternatively, they may move between organisations whilst undertaking these different roles. Either way, the likelihood of any employee remaining in standard full-time employment for their whole working life is diminishing rapidly.

Chapter 11

Organisational Restructuring

More than ever before, change is a constant presence in today's workplace. New technology, skills and markets, investor and competitor pressures, legislation and trade agreements – the list of factors seems almost endless and the speed with which they affect organisations is increasing. All of these are bound to have an impact on your organisation which will require structural modifications from time to time.

However, successful implementation of corporate plans requires not just a structure and communication of intentions, but also management of the resources needed to deliver them – as currently envisaged and within the possible range of variations that can be foreseen. Many of these are described in the next chapter but, they are by definition very difficult to predict accurately and therefore to plan for with any certainty. Nevertheless, it is perfectly possible to cost the impact of *failing* to deliver corporate plans – always assuming that the organisation remains in operation if the failure is severe.

In most organisations, the greatest significant factor will be the need to have the right staff in the right place at the right time. Effective manpower planning can minimise the costs of change and help develop contingency plans. Valid decision-making requires easy access to trends and forecasts, as well as to current information on:

- what human resources are available when
- what skills and experience they possess
- how and where these skills can be effectively deployed
- what training might be required from where
- what contingency options are available if key staff leave.

As discussed in previous chapters, analysis of local productivity levels, absenteeism and labour turnover may also indicate further options. A computerised system, providing accurate and timely information, can help quickly to identify missing or misplaced resources. It should also be able to model alternative options, showing the effect of changed structures on every aspect of the HR remit – including the costs of change due to whatever mix is required of redundancies, relocation, recruitment, training and so on.

Whilst it is impossible to put an average cost on the lack of adequate resource plans, the huge impact of any *delay* in implementing the corporate plans can be shown (at least in broad outline) very quickly.

BASE ASSUMPTIONS used for purposes of illustration only:

Current number of full-time employees	= 500
Current sales revenue per employee	= £50,000
Current average weekly wage	= £250
Current non-wage expenditure budget	= 64% × revenue
Current gross operating profit	= £2.5m
Planned reduction in full-time employees	= 10%
Planned increase in turnover per employee	= 20%
Planned average weekly wage	= £275
Planned non-wage expenditure budget	= 60% × revenue
Planned gross operating profit	= £4.365m
Monthly cost of delayed implementation	= £155,417

Even without accounting for the cost of corrections if implementation is imperfect, each month of delay will severely dent the profit target. A basic model (p. 87) demonstrates the scale of the opportunity – or risk.

On the assumptions stated, and assuming a near-immediate improvement in profitability if the changes are fully implemented, the cost of each full month's delay in achieving the new objectives could exceed £150,000. Even this isn't the full story, since the model has assumed that all changes are taking place in isolation from outside interference – or at least that such factors have been accounted for within the new operating plan and targets. If one of the driving forces for the new plan involves a takeover or merger, whether instigated or being fought off by your organisation, the damage caused by delay in implementation may prove fatal in the longer term.

Although the necessary investment to carry through the planned changes, therefore, is demonstrably critical, the job for HR is not over. You will still need to show the relevance of your proposals, possibly by using some of the previous models or variations thereon, but it should now prove simple to answer any questions as to their value. If you want to take a more proactive approach to involving HR in the business plans for your organisation, then the next section of this book should help to build on the examples given so far.

Sample Form for Calculation

Costing current operations

Enter number of employees   _____ (a),

Enter sales revenue per employee   £ _____ (b),

Multiply (a) x (b)   £ _____ (c) = Annual turnover

Enter average weekly wage   £ _____ (d),

Multiply (a) x (d) x 52   £ _____ (e),

Enter non-wage expenditure/revenue   _____ % (f),

Multiply (c) x (f)   £ _____ (g),

Add (e) + (g)   £ _____ (h) = Annual costs

Calculate [(c) − (h)]/(c)   _____ % (i) = Operating margin

Multiply (c) x (i)   £ _____ (j) = *Profit before tax*

Costing delayed change

Enter planned headcount reduction   _____ % (k),

Enter planned increase in revenue

     per employee   _____ % (l),

Multiply (a) x [100.0 − (k)]/100   _____ (m),

Multiply (b) x [100.0 + (l)]/100   £ _____ (n),

Multiply (m) x (n)   £ _____ (o) = New annual turnover

Enter planned weekly wage increase   _____ % (p),

Multiply (d) x [100.0 + (p)]/100   £ _____ (q),

Multiply (m) x (q) x 52   £ _____ (r),

Enter planned non-wage

     expenditure/revenue   _____ % (s),

Multiply (o) x (s)   £ _____ (t),

Add (r) + (t)   £ _____ (u) = New annual costs

Calculate [(o) − (u)]/(o)   _____ % (v) = New operating margin

Multiply (o) x (v)   £ _____ (w) = *New profit before tax*

Calculate [(w) − (j)]/12.0   £ _____ (x) = *Monthly cost of*
                                                        delayed implementation

PART THREE:
DECISIONS, DECISIONS

Every function in an organisation is, and should be, increasingly reviewed in terms of the value of its contribution to strategic objectives. Personnel, as one of the service suppliers rather than a direct revenue generator, is having to demonstrate not only that it is effective but that it provides real value for money.

This can be difficult to achieve when many people find it hard to quantify the questions they want to ask, let alone give accurate answers. In the previous section, we focussed on sizing the cost of various areas within the remit of Personnel. There is, however, always the danger that a mass of detail will obscure the most fundamental fact – that employee-related costs are often the single biggest item of expenditure for an organisation.

This is not just a matter of salaries. In the extreme case of service industries, it is easy to show the massive disparity between direct paybill costs and the actual cost per 'output' employee (i.e. those delivering the end-result service). For instance, the most recent published figures show that the basic pay for a Police Constable in Britain averages out at about £17,000 p.a. However, the Audit Commission has recently claimed that each visible police presence on the street costs £550,000 p.a. – or over 30 times basic salary. Similar figures have been quoted for nurses, with a basic salary of just over £12,000 p.a. upon qualifying, although the annual cost per nurse of providing direct care to patients on wards for 24 hours per day comes to some £300,000 p.a.

It should now be obvious why headcount is often used as a basic indicator of an organisation's costs. However, such figures can be dangerous if the assumptions and details behind the calculations are not known, or where statistics are twisted for political or other purposes. It might seem tempting to say that a Constable's daily 'rate' of £1,500 for an all-week presence is exorbitant and could be reduced. But, as with nurses, the essential nature of the public service provided means that costs are incurred for facilities that may only be required occasionally. These might not be justified by a more profit-driven organisation, but you try explaining that to someone in need of emergency assistance.

The key for all organisations lies not in assuming that reductions in expenditure are desirable in themselves but in ensuring that costs are applied practically and effectively. Since so many of them have a large HR element, it is critical that Personnel becomes truly integrated with all the other business-planning functions.

In so doing, it is important to remember that the application of short-term financial objectives may be misleading unless seen in the context of longer-term strategies. Before you rush into decisions based on financial ratios and models, remind yourself of the original objectives. Avoid simplistic assessments like appearing to save costs by freezing recruitment or attempting automatically to increase productivity by spending more money.

If you have read earlier chapters carefully, you should now be in a position to know where the opportunities are to be found and to justify the appropriate actions. But there are still some major issues to be considered before decisions are taken and commitments made.

For a start, there is the whole question of the financial relationship between the Personnel function and the rest of the organisation. Are you a central function, acting as custodian of corporate budgets? This will encourage the view that the costs of the department are part of general overheads, which puts you right in the firing line for short-term cutbacks whenever these are demanded.

Have you made the move, voluntarily or otherwise, to re-charging any other departments for your services? Whether such contracting out is a book-keeping exercise or in full competition with external suppliers, it allows many of your costs to be directly associated with other departments. In theory, you should even be able to get a 'sales' forecast of their requirements on which to plan your own resources – including any sub-contracting of specialist work.

Are you prepared to go as far as a few management consultancies and charge for your services, but only on a 'results' basis – taking your fee as a cut of the extra profits generated or savings achieved? To the best of my knowledge this approach has never been attempted by an in-house function and is not being seriously recommended. The point, though, is that your relationship with the rest of the organisation can span the whole range from dependence to independence. Its position should be a deliberate strategy, which then determines your use of the financial framework for HR.

Serious consideration should also be given to another factor. All the exercises so far have concentrated on measuring costs (and changes in them) based on one massive assumption. Namely that the organisation has remained impervious to change during the period for which data has been collected.

At the most basic level, if the period in question is around 3 years or longer, you may need to make some adjustments for inflation, since the value of the £s invested will not equate to the purchasing power of the £s saved in later years. There is no point in predicting savings of £20,000 (at current prices) over 3 years, if the initial investment required is £15,000 and inflation is running at 10% p.a. in each of the 3 years. The apparent benefit to the organisation becomes transformed from a gain of £5,000 (or a 33% return) to a gain of £35 (a 0.23% return) – which is unlikely to warrant the effort involved. There are, of course, many other potential change factors, to which we turn in the next chapter.

Chapter 12

The Continuum of Changing Factors

One of the major difficulties in achieving corporate plans is ensuring that the right people are in the right place at the right time. Change is a constant factor today and is always costly, even where the eventual outcome is planned profits.

Human resource or manpower planning is critical to the chances of successfully implementing the corporate plan. It is also an effective way of minimising the costs of change and ensuring the existence of contingency plans. Planned results are delivered by people, so any missing or misplaced resources seriously delay or damage the original intentions. In the current economic climate, few corporate plans can absorb the resulting shortfalls.

As a simple exercise, look back to the last time your organisation made changes to its operating plan – whether this was exceptional or part of a normal review. Somewhere at the heart of the plan there will be a clear target for increased revenues, reduced costs or some other quantifiable output that can be expressed as a financial value. Now, if the plan was due to be implemented at the beginning of Quarter 3, the cost of a one-month delay is equivalent to at least a sixth (and probably far more) of the intended benefits for that financial year. If those benefits were worthwhile in the first place, that delay is going to represent a considerable sum – much greater than any costs saved by not recruiting/training/relocating staff within the timescale required by the plan.

The graph shown in Figure 18 shows a typical example of how a project moves over time, from pure cost through payback and into profit. During the first phase only costs are incurred, then returns (whether revenue or projected savings) start to come in; at first they do not even cover the continuing costs, but slowly they build up to the point where they exceed current costs and accumulated costs-to-date are being paid-off. Once the initial deficit is removed, the project has achieved payback and will start to show a real profit. On this basis, you can see that a one-month delay in starting the project may cause an apparently very different result at the end of the financial year. Starting on schedule enables payback to be achieved during the current fiscal year and is therefore attractive, whilst a delayed start would result in the project showing a net loss at the year-end.

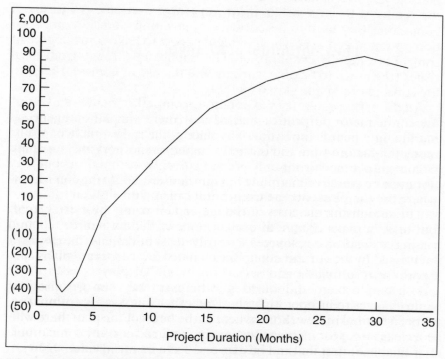

Figure 18   Cumulative Cash Flow on a Typical Project

Implementing change, however, is not merely a mechanistic exercise. The resilience of the organisation to change is ultimately determined by the resilience of its human resources. The Personnel function, therefore, has a unique opportunity to be the agent of change, since it will have the only complete view of all the factors affecting the human resources. What is not so easy to obtain is an equivalent grasp of the *external* factors of change affecting your organisation, yet before a start is made on reorganising the workforce, or any of its practices, some account must be taken of the potential impact of such factors on your assumptions.

The rate of change in most of these areas is acclerating so, even if you are less than fully scientific in quantifying each one, some compensation or contingency needs to be built into your plans. Six main areas are particularly worth considering.

Globalisation

Despite all the talk about the effects of the European Single Market, the reality is far less localised for most organisations. *All* forms of boundaries that used to describe the area within which an organisation operated and over which it might expect to have some degree of control are rapidly evaporating. The implications range from local issues (the move to flexible working and the use of homeworkers) to the concept of a single global market.

All the earlier references to obtaining competitor figures and ratios for comparative purposes assumed that there was a homogeneous market in which competition was taking place. In practice, whilst many threats are from established competitors, others may emanate from companies who not only are not currently competitors but may not even be perceived as being in your market. So if you don't know where the threat may come from, what can you do about it?

The reasons for the arrival of a major new competitor are varied, but often a sharp change in one or more of the costs of production (materials and/or employees) is involved. Whilst such changes may be caused by one of the other factors listed later in this chapter, the opportunity provided and seized on by global players is to move production around the world to wherever they can get the best returns on a reduced cost-base. This can mean your current competitors allocating work on a project-by-project basis or to widely dispersed but specialist manufacturing and sub-assembly locations. For instance, despite the logistics and scale of project management required, most of the oil-rigs in the North Sea were designed and assembled in between 5 and 8 different countries.

New competitors will also be attracted by the opportunity to compete with a lower cost-base, whether they are brand new organisations or diversification for an international company established in a different market. If their quality is comparable (or better) and their unit production costs sufficiently low to compensate for distribution delays and costs, then you will eventually lose business to them.

This does not apply just to manufacturing industries like shipbuilding and motorcycles. The global market now also affects the provision of services, as can be seen in the fight for market share between the various Stock Exchanges around the world. Another example which would have been unthinkable even a few years ago concerns large software development projects. Several UK companies are currently experimenting with programming services supplied from India and the Far East. Whilst the project management costs are higher than usual, it is believed that the low-cost skilled programmers in these countries can not only reduce overall project costs but deliver a higher quality product – which in turn typically reduces any reworking costs.

In the example shown in Figure 19, the unit development cost is forecast to be ⅓ lower if carried out at location B despite increases in transport and project management costs. If the unit selling price was £900, this would translate into an increase of nearly 50% in the gross margin available to your organisation.

	Location A £	Location B £
Employee costs	315	165
Bought in materials	50	55
Spoilage/re-working	94.5	24.7
Transport	4	12
Project management	63	94.5
Contingency expenses	10	10
Total/Unit	536.5	361.2

Notes: the cost of associated time and materials for documentation and other UK activities are not included; development costs are assumed to be apportioned across 1,000 units of production.

Figure 19   Unit Development Costs in Different Locations

The other side of these international cost issues is the opportunity to do business in more countries. Whilst it is only one factor, if you know which countries have a noticeably higher unit production cost than your own, then you have a potential export market to investigate. So what you need to do is to identify the major components of your unit production costs and then determine which are to some extent under your control – as opposed to those for which you can only make allowances in your plans.

Those that form some part of the labour cost can then be quantified and analysed as discussed earlier in this book. Don't forget, though, that your responsibility for the HR element is not suddenly restricted to direct costs. You may propose moving a production unit whose output is critical to other parts of the business (and hence completion of saleable products) to an area with 30% lower labour costs. Yet even if this is financially justified, after allowing for costs of materials and distribution, you will not be thanked for overlooking other productivity factors – such as a local tendency to hold unofficial fiestas every fortnight during working hours or a general history of industrial unrest.

The Economy

One of the least predictable factors that can nevertheless have a dramatic impact on any financially based plan is a major change in the economy – whether national or global. If you know consistently and accurately how to foretell events like the stock market crash in 1987 or the duration of every recession, then you have greater opportunities open to you than this book can unveil.

If, however, like the rest of us, you can make no such claim, then all you can do is take the advice of the various professionals with relevant skills and knowledge – whether specialists like econometricians or, more typically, whoever in your Finance department is prepared to help. All you are looking for is the range of values which you should assume for the key financial variables used within your models (e.g. forecast exchange rates if employees are being paid in more than one currency; projected inflation rates and subsidies available in different countries, etc). These can be used to determine the degree of risk inherent in your plan, rather than to validate or reject it outright.

Technology

Many advances in technology bring only miniscule improvements to current production or operating procedures and their impact is limited to providing an extra edge or margin. Less often, but with increasing regularity, a new technology provides a complete step change to the way we do things – or even makes possible a complete new industry.

The historical example most frequently used is invention of steam-powered engines, which provided the basis for the industrial revolution in the latter half of the 18th century. Within a very short space of time, a large percentage of the population moved from agrarian or home-based working to employment in purpose-built factories that could achieve economies of scale previously unimagined.

Others may disagree, but I believe the next two most important technological revolutions have been in this century: international transport and the PC (personal computer). Both share a common characteristic, that they make communication virtually independent of distance and time – indeed they are what has enabled the previously mentioned globalisation of markets. They also both, and particularly the microchip, have an impact on the rate of change affecting your organisation.

Although you can find chips in almost everything now – from time and attendance machines to faxes, telephones and photocopiers – it is the PC that has revolutionised (and will continue to revolutionise) two key aspects of most organisations. The result has been an improved information base and considerably faster communication channels.

Neither of these has an immediate effect on the *structure* of the models you have been creating, but they provide the opportunity to analyse many more variations and options and raise the expectation of a far more rapid response to the other factors of change. They also impose certain modifications in working practices and skill requirements, but in this context that is less relevant than managing any information overload -- often caused by the demand for instant general reports rather than a focussed selection of data.

Cultures

Sometimes described as the commonly accepted way in which things get done, culture is not restricted to factors internal to the organisation. Changes in the political agenda of the ruling party in any country inevitably set in motion changes in the general culture – although whether in tune with or in opposition to their plans is less predictable.

Many of these deliberate changes will be specifically targeted at aspects of employment, often for demographic reasons, and may have a huge impact on Personnel. Less obvious elements of a political agenda, however, can have just as important a bearing on your business strategies and thence on your HR objectives. For instance, the recent trend towards privatisation of public utilities means that they are now more open to alternative suppliers of raw materials. Whether you agree or disagree with this approach, it can mean life or death to your company if you are involved in the production or transportation of such materials.

There are, of course, many other cultural differences such as those based on national or religious grounds that will impact on your HR plans – particularly if you are trying to manage (or at least co-ordinate) an international workforce in many countries. The remuneration mix, for example, will be as affected by cultural attitudes to performance pay as by the local cost of living.

A more light-hearted example relates to the incredible variety of public holidays in different countries. Every December for the last 5 years I have seen quotes in the newspapers from senior US executives saying they 'are staggered at the way that the UK seems to shut down for up to 10 days over Christmas'. A brief study reveals the more complex truth behind the inference that the English are lazier than Americans; in England we have only 9 public holidays in 1992, compared to 18 in the USA although we tend to be granted longer paid holidays. In fact, excluding the former Iron Curtain countries, England and Ireland have the least public holidays of all European countries, as can be seen on the graph in Figure 20. This becomes a serious issue when you are calculating daily employee costs, based on the number of days for which they are available, for use in productivity ratios and unit costs.

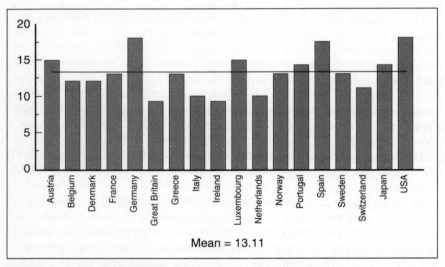

Mean = 13.11

Figure 20   Number of Public Holidays in 1992

It is also advisable to bear in mind the sheer diversity of dates on which one or more countries are celebrating a public holiday. Analysis of the major industrialised nations in Europe shows that 35% of all working days (Monday to Friday) are a public holiday in at least one country. Even more pertinent, if for instance you are planning a multinational recruitment campaign, is to try to avoid the period from April to June when this 'unavailability' rate rises to 66%. (Traditional times for summer holidays obviously become a key factor later in the year.)

Demography

In theory, one of the easier rates of change to predict should be the effect of local demographic patterns. Without descending to actuarial depths of accuracy, the main trends are fairly evident from publicly available statistics and they are often commented on avidly in the press.

The best-known current example is the falling number of young people in the Western world entering the employment market every year. The effect on your plans, however, is less easy to predict. It was not long ago that it was being quoted as the basis for a recruitment crisis. Although a few organisations with both a sound financial base and a long-term vision of employee development are still concerned by this factor, the majority do not see recruitment either as a priority or as difficult to complete when required.

These rather global statements obviously hide more prosaic concerns at the local level. The total number of people in the employment market may not be of great significance to you if a substantial majority of your needs are based on specific skills or qualifications that are in relatively short supply. In some industries demographic factors may have a greater effect on staff turnover and the leavers' profile. Thus an increase in the average age of management is being experienced in industries (such as computing) which have no previous experience of this or suitable policies in place.

The impact of demographic change is usually exceedingly complex, due to the interaction of all the other factors. For instance, advances in technology typically alter the demand for skills far more quickly than any change in their availability; sourcing them from a wider (non-national) pool may then require changes in local practices to accommodate a common framework. A most extreme and sad example of wrongly basing strategies on a single strand of demography was the focus given at the beginning of 1990 to addressing an envisaged shortage of new employees. The effect of economic changes in the form of high (and rising) unemployment soon negated many of the underlying assumptions.

Cultural change can also be attributed directly to shifts in the economy as government initiatives are given more credence, or expectations of protection by employers disappear. Similarly, the retreat by many organisations from a commitment to equal opportunity policies was largely predictable. Since the real (rather than espoused) motive was recruiting resources that were unavailable elsewhere, the disappearance of such shortages has often coincided with the policies not being implemented.

All these arguments show the immense difficulties of making predictions based on demographics. Although they may seem the most accessible of the change factors at work, they are likely to be most relevant (for the purposes of creating financial models) as *secondary* influences on the other factors mentioned in this chapter.

Legislation

Despite the substantial body of employment legislation that exists in the UK, remarkably little of it makes a *direct* contribution to employee costs. The more obvious areas, such as National Insurance levies, are generally reviewed annually – and rarely result in a reduction in costs for employers. Whilst precise predictions cannot be made, the size of any change can be allowed for with a reasonable degree of confidence.

There are other comparable areas that are often treated as totally unpredictable, but actually show clear evidence of a trend. One example would be the evolution of SSP (Statutory Sickness Pay) legislation since its inception nearly 10 years ago. Initially employers were made responsible for the administration of payments for the first 8 weeks of sickness, but this was extended in 1985 to cover the first 28 weeks. This was described as getting employers to process such payments 'on behalf of the state' (a full refund was always obtainable) with the aim of reducing the state's administrative burden. At first this led to complaint from employers (particularly in small businesses) that it involved an increase in their operating costs – from administration and from funding the cashflow.

As might have been predicted, however, an underlying trend had been set in motion of moving away from government responsibility for funding payments during an employee's period of sickness. This is now properly evidenced by the 1991 Bill, which restricts the amount of SSP that is reclaimable by employers to 80%. In the short term, this has led to some creative responses from hard-pressed employers. One example is the remarkable increase in sicknesses being reported for Saturdays and Sundays. This is, of course, totally unrelated to a basic mathematical realisation: that if an employee who is paid £50 per day is off sick on Monday and Tuesday, his or her employer can only reclaim £16.80 (i.e. 80% of $2/5 \times$ £52.50, the higher weekly SSP rate). If, however, the employee happens to claim that their sickness started on the Sunday, then the employer can expect a refund of £25.20, thus compensating for the 80% rate.

This example of changes in SSP may or may not foreshadow a general transfer of welfare payments from state to employer. It seems less likely with maternity and industrial injury benefits, although a similar trend appears to have started with responsibility for state pensions being transferred more to employees. In every case there will be a knock-on effect on employee costs, either direct or via more adventurous remuneration and benefits packages. The provision of occupational sick pay schemes, for instance, is becoming far more prevalent, but it always carries a high cost.

Whether this is merely ideologically driven or a necessary move towards employer accountability, it seems clear that employers can expect to shoulder more financial liabilities for each and every employee. Where these include employees on overseas employment contracts, different but similar issues will arrive. For instance, in the United States the high cost of medical services and lack of a proper national programme means that health care is a substantial element of employee costs. It may, therefore, be sensible to show alternative assumptions for the breakdown of employee costs when building the models described in earlier chapters.

All the change factors described have one common feature – they are independent of the organisation and so cannot be directly controlled. There are, however, many changes which are totally within the remit of the organisation. The validity of the strategic options that these represent can often be dependent on HR issues.

The Time Factor

When evaluating possible new products or markets, the initial emphasis is invariably on the potential scale of opportunity. If this looks at all attractive, then the question of whether the organisation is in a position to supply it profitably becomes the key. This, of course, means that strategic HR decisions can be applied even to individual projects. Suppose that the Board wants a new product, Marketing has confirmed the potential and Sales are prepared to commit to revenues from the day that the product is launched. The Production director estimates that it will take 6 months to gear up for full production – but only if sufficient, correctly trained staff are in place in 10 weeks' time.

When translated into detailed recruitment and training plans and these are costed out, there will be considerable pressure to cut the proposed budgets or to delay the expenditure 'just for a few weeks'. The kind of 'report' shown in Figure 21 is a powerful way of demonstrating the additional cost of either of these indecisive options. Scenario A assumes that all necessary resources are in place at the start of production and that revenues therefore start in July and increase at a steady monthly rate for the first year. The differences in scenario B are that, due to resources being phased in, sales start a month later and achieve a slightly lower rate of growth in August and September, before catching up with the rate shown in scenario A.

As can be seen, the cumulative difference is substantial. Scenario A contributes revenues of £521,000 in the current financial year (ending 1 April), while scenario B delivers only £292,000 – or nearly £0.25 million less. Depending on the intended shelf-life of the product, the net result could even mean that the project ceases to be viable.

Other factors might include a smaller eventual market-share due to entering it later than competitors and/or the additional costs of maintaining older products that are needed to retain acceptable revenues until the new product launch. None of this is justification for *carte blanche* investment in every opportunity, but it does show that the cost of not properly funding a committed project will far outweigh the attempted savings. Should this approach show the

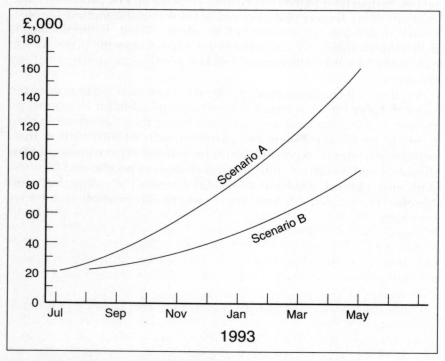

Figure 21   New Product Monthly Revenue Forecasts

opposite, that the delays are worthwhile, it would also suggest that you should carefully re-evaluate the profit potential of the whole project.

As I have tried to demonstrate throughout this chapter, there is no static equilibrium in any model that perfectly reflects a business or its human resources. But although many external factors bias the data and/or affect the models, it is the general impact that you need to understand rather than precise forecasts. Indeed this is where the right kind of models, and the use of computers, can really make a difference. An iterative approach to building the models allows them to evolve from your experience, slowly coming to represent more and more the unique properties of your organisation. Re-checking with alternative sets of data can also allow you to test the impact of outside influences and trends. It can even make clear cyclical effects based on the calendar or changes in fashion – and then make allowances for them.

It is not going to be possible for you to quantify all these change factors properly, let alone every time you cost an HR proposal, since many of them deserve and have whole books (and sometimes professions) dedicated to understanding them. What is important is sufficient awareness of their potential impact on your plans so you can make suitable allowances (and/or contigencies) when setting them out.

So, if not all change is predictable, what can be done to reduce the risks and give you that edge? It is no more possible for Personnel on its own to solve the strategic problems facing their organisation than it would be for the Finance department without information from other departments. Access to and management of information across divisions and countries, plus the integration of people and business data into a knowledge base shared fully across the enterprise, must become the objective. And that is where information technology comes in.

Chapter 13

Technology for Decision Support

T. S. Eliot once asked 'Where is the knowledge we have lost in information?' Although his question was philosophical in intent, the sentiment may be echoed in many Boardrooms. 'Information overload' is a modern phrase that you may have come across. It sometimes refers to the chaos that naive computer-users can create when they confuse vast amounts of data with useful information. However, it can just as often refer to the result of capable but over-enthusiastic computer users who generate so much information that they can no longer remember the original objectives. Yet even when neither of these excesses occur, the sheer volume of data and rate of change reported can mean that the human mind is no longer capable of responding in a sensible way. The systems now used by Stock Exchanges are a perfect example – they have had to hand over some of the decision-making process to the computers themselves.

So, with all these potential dangers, not to mention the lurid newspaper headlines about viruses and hacking, why should you be expected to be enthusiastic about using information technology (IT) in the personnel department? The answer, of course, is that IT (like any other business tool) can be introduced and used effectively – or misunderstood and abused. Ensuring its effectiveness requires the same basic rules as apply to all major new projects: identifying clear objectives, quantifying the resources necessary to achieve them, following the implementation through and then reviewing the process for potential areas to improve. Lack of consensus on the original objective or a loss of focus to follow an interesting but irrelevant alternative are the commonest causes of failure. All this is discussed in detail in Alastair Evans's excellent *Computers and Personnel Systems* (IPM, 1991), but the basic principles are fairly straightforward.

Typically, there are three main phases of implementing IT in an organisation:

i) *direct support for the individual*, which used to mean providing regular reports or occasionally access to the mainframe via a terminal. The rapid fall in hardware prices increasingly means that individuals now have access to a PC (personal computer). These can improve personal productivity but do not share information or communicate with anyone else.

ii) *departmental shared systems*, where more than one person in the department can access the same system at the same time. The pooled information has a far more pronounced effect on productivity and allows different people to be involved on a single project (e.g. in recruitment).

iii) *enterprise-wide integration*, where systems from different departments are interlinked so that common data can be held once but still feed many areas. This phase has been properly achieved so far by only a few organisations, but it is the key to effective business leverage through IT.

The primary benefit from all three phases is the sheer speed at which certain functions can be processed. Basic examples include dealing with simple ad-hoc enquiries (is the suspicious looking car outside a staff vehicle?) or printing personal letters to all the applicants for a job on the same day. When phase two is reached, the bigger benefit comes from consistency of data. Nothing will destroy the credibility of personnel more quickly than different headcount figures in reports produced by two people in the same department – not uncommon with either manual systems or multiple unintegrated computer systems.

The final phase should bring the ultimate objective at least in sight, where every person in the organisation has direct access to all data relevant to their job. The complete integration of systems means that the same data may be viewed in great detail on the shopfloor or appear as a hidden element in a graphical forecast seen by the Board. The rate of implementation of this approach is not only dependent on innovation and cost reduction in technology, but on cultural changes towards acceptance of open access to information. It does not mean that all information is available to everyone, but it does encourage greater communication generally. It is assumed at this stage that most readers will either have or be considering the introduction of computers within the Personnel department, but that this will currently be only at phase one or two.

At first sight, it should be fairly simple to acquire or build a system on a PC that holds a database of basic information for each employee (name, address, job, pay-rate, length of service, marital status, etc). But the range of useful information is enormous and much of it changes over time, so you will need to capture these changes and retain a record of previous data in such a way that you can easily report on any selection or combination of them.

Another key aspect is validation of the data being input, whether at the keyboard or via electronic links from other systems (such as time and attendance machines), to ensure that it is sensible. If you are allowed to enter someone's job as Makreting Executive, then they will not be included in any reports on people with Marketing in their job title. Also, most data is related in one way or another to other items; organisational structures and all such relationships must be properly defined and enforced by the system. For instance, booking someone on a training course should automatically deduct the cost from the relevant budget and signal the need for an evaluation to be entered after the course finishes.

Once you move to a departmental solution (often referred to as a multi-user system) you will see even more clearly how every item of data may be re-used time after time by several people. If you enter the cost of a recruitment advertisement on your system, for example, it may be included later (visibly or otherwise) within:

- the annual cost of all recruitment advertising
- the cost of all recruitment for one department
- the replacement costs for one particular job

and any of 20 or more categories. And yet, despite all this, you will also want to retain full control over who has access to what data – both in terms of what they can see and what they can enter or change. As you can see, setting up – let alone building – such a system is not an inconsiderable task. But it should not be particularly daunting if you approach it as a project in itself. Your main objectives, short and medium term, can be identified and quantified. To begin with, you may want to concentrate on building a basic recording system, before moving on to graphical reports and then models to test 'what if' scenarios (such as alternative pay awards). Try to define any current procedures and policies you already operate and where you most want to improve the services that you provide. Remember that the structure you set up will ultimately control what you can easily do with your system (although you should be able to change it later if necessary).

You are now in a position to consider how much it is worth spending to achieve these objectives – and to evaluate alternative options, such as whether to build the system within your organisation or buy it in as a software package. Again, Alastair Evans's *Computers and Personnel Systems* offers much useful guidance, but the basic situation is similar to the ones you found yourself in earlier chapters, when you identified an HR strategy and its potential savings for the organisation. You know it makes sense and can place a value on it, but you still have to convince the relevant people to free up or even create a budget from which to fund proposals which unfortunately attract implementation costs before any payback can be achieved.

The temptation is to guess at a budget which will easily support your claim for quick payback, but this is very short-sighted. Any problems you experience in getting a budget approved will be nothing compared to the pressures applied if you return for further top-ups that are not demonstrably beyond your control (and these are few). You should be prepared to spend as much time estimating your costs as in quantifying the potential savings – making sure that you are looking at all the project costs, not just the more visible ones.

So, once the intention to invest in a computer system has been reached, the first step is to evaluate the possible costs involved. For instance, it may initially seem tempting to have the system written specially for you by your IT or MIS department. But what is often forgotten is that writing software is only a small part of the complex process that eventually leads to an operational system. It is also prone to overrunning budgets and missing delivery deadlines.

Key elements usually underestimated or even left out include:

- scope, specification and design stages
- prototype and main software development
- alpha and beta-testing, release and installation
- re-engineering, re-release and re-installation
- technical, user and training documentation
- product training and (helpdesk) support
- product maintenance for bugs/reliability
- product enhancements for new applications
- product changes due to external forces
- continuous system supervision/housekeeping.

There is also an extended learning curve when testing the new system, since there is no previous experience available. And any calls for support or maintenance will have to compete with other corporate priorities. Given an average cost of from £200 per day for the skilled professionals involved, a fairly basic system can often finish up costing over £100,000 just to develop – and much more to support and maintain.

A proven software package, however, is designed to deal with all these processes and amortises the costs across all its users. The direct savings thereby gained can be substantially magnified by the costs of getting it wrong or late through in-house development. Maintenance, support and training will be priority services from a package supplier with the experience to help you when trying out new applications.

If software is regarded as a capital investment with a presumed shelf life of, say, 4 years, then it can be seen that a package solution may bring substantial cost savings – without compromising the quality or durability of the system. Applying the same format as when looking at various HR applications earlier, you can create a model of the cost factors involved in developing and running your system and then compare it to the alternative of buying a commercially supported package. As before, the example on pp. 110–11 does not claim to be comprehensive and can be amended or added to, to suit your particular circumstances.

For instance, it can be finetuned by using per-day costs of real individuals or, for instance, by applying discounted cash flow to the annual running costs. Discounted cash flow (DCF) examines cash inflows and outflows (rather than revenues, costs and profits) and then applies discounts to reflect the cost of money and the degree of risk involved. You might even ask the IT department to quote in this format if they are recharging you for on-going services as well as development projects. It would not be uncommon, depending on the scale of your requirements, to find the in-house solution costing between 2 and 5 times as much as the bought-in package – and considerably more in some cases.

Whatever the other competing claims made by your IT department or a package supplier, there should be no doubt that you need a stable and rugged system. If crucial decisions based on answers gained from the system are to be taken quickly and with confidence as to the accuracy of the data, you don't want to be wasting unnecessary time on repairs to your database.

No attempt has been made to quantify the level of improved efficiency and morale often found within the Personnel department itself or to put a value on the power of easily understood and timely graphical reports. All the focus has been on direct operational savings, since ultimately no computer-based information system can generate direct savings. It is merely the technology that enables improved decision-making through accurate information.

What is certain is that lack of this information precludes effective personnel management – and has a detrimental impact on the bottom line. Few organisations would question the need to computerise their Finance function and equally few *should* question the computerisation of information which helps them control their most costly resource. You may think that information is expensive – but lack of it will not prove a low-cost alternative.

Being competitive means reacting quickly to change, and preferably being there first, which requires accurate and timely personnel information on which to base quality decisions. The IT system should also help you to monitor the effectiveness of your implementation strategies, the most common area of weakness in the corporate plan.

A lot of effort has been expended in recent years by organisations in an attempt to quantify the real value of IT and its contribution to the bottom line. So far there have been few claims that this can be clearly demonstrated, although failures generally have less to do with the technology or people using it than with the lack of a strategy. Concentrating on what the organisation *needs* to achieve before you decide *how* to do it may sound obvious, but it is remarkably uncommon.

A few computer systems can be justified simply because they are an intrinsic part of the production process or interacting with customers. A personnel system, like other management information systems, must add to the productivity of management by delivering quantifiable improvements in decisions and controls. The HR function has an edge here since, as shown in previous chapters, it is possible to draw a direct connection between the uses of personnel information and contribution to profits.

It is also just as possible to use it to determine possible values within a comprehensive corporate business model. For instance, most organisations will have an (annual) operating plan showing, amongst other items, projected revenue-lines and cost-lines. If the revenue actually obtained in a particular month is less than forecast, then the first question will be whether this results from a one-off cause or represents a decrement in the median revenue-line for the year. In the latter case, you can expect some requests for alternative HR costs based on a wide range of possible scenarios.

A word of warning should be borne in mind whatever the circumstances. Be careful of deliberate fraud – usually described as 'possibly undue optimism' by the perpetrator when discovered. I am not referring to fraud in the criminal sense, although the effects can be even more devastating to the organisation. The quality of reports generated by computers can allow the unscrupulous to assume, often correctly, that they will be read as gospel. This is the same as the 'if it's in the newspaper, it must be true' syndrome. The manipulation may be a slight change in assumptions or wholesale alteration of data, but careful checking for anomalies with previous reports should prevent you being caught out.

Sample Form for Calculation

Costing an in-house IT solution

Enter average true cost of IT staff
    per man-day   £ _____ (a),

Enter days for scope analysis   _____ (b),
Enter days for project specification   _____ (c),
Enter days for system design/analysis   _____ (d),
Multiply (a) x [(b) + (c) + (d)]   £ _____ (e)   = Pre-development

Enter days for prototype development   _____ (f),
Enter days for further programming   _____ (g),
Multiply (a) x [(f) + (g)]   £ _____ (h)   = Development Part I

Enter days for alpha- and beta-testing   _____ (i),
Enter days for release handover   _____ (j),
Enter days for system installation   _____ (k),
Multiply (a) x [(i) + (j) + (k)]   £ _____ (l)   = Testing Part I

Enter days for re-engineering product   _____ (m),
Multiply (a) x (m)   £ _____ (n)   = Development Part II

Enter days for repeat of beta-testing   _____ (o),
Enter days for re-release handover   _____ (p),
Enter days for system re-installation   _____ (q),
Multiply (a) x [(o) + (p) + (q)]   £ _____ (r)   = Testing Part II

Enter days for programme documentation _____ (s),
Enter days for user manual/documentation _____ (t),
Enter days for creating training course
    materials   _____ (u),
Multiply (a) x [(s) + (t) + (u)]   £ _____ (v)   = Documentation

Enter days for product training courses   _____ (w),
Enter days for product/helpdesk support _____ (x),
Enter days for system supervision   _____ (y),
Multiply (a) x [(w) + (x) + (y)]   £ _____ (z)   = Operating support

Enter days for product error correction   _____ (2),
Enter days for applications enhancement   _____ (3),
Enter days for other product changes   _____ (4),
Multiply (a) x [(2) + (3) + (4)]   £ _____ (5),

Enter frequency of product changes p.a. _____ (6),

Multiply (6) x (r)   £_____ (7),

Add (5) + (7)   £_____ (8) = Maintenance

Add (e)+(h)+(l)+(n)+(r)+(v)   £_____ (9) = Upfront costs

Enter shelf-life of product (years)   _____ (10),

Multiply [(z) + (8)] x (10)   £_____ (11) = Running costs

Add (9) + (11)   £_____ (12) = *Project cost*

Costing a commercial package solution

Software licence/purchase costs   £_____ (13) = Upfront costs

Enter cost per day of training courses £_____ (14),

Enter days for product training course   _____ (15),

Enter annual maintenance/helpline fee £_____ (16),

Enter shelf-life of product (years)   _____ (17),

Add [(14) x (15)] + [(16) x (17)]   £_____ (18) = Running costs

Add (13) + (18)   £_____ (19) = *Project cost*

Chapter 14

A Temporary Conclusion?

Right at the beginning of this book I stated that one of the key objectives of following the approach set out here was to enable you to become involved in strategic decision-making processes within your organisation. This will be fully achieved only if you raise consciousness of and belief in your HR strategy to the point where it is an integral part of the corporate strategy and not just an adjunct to it.

Any strategy must be founded on helping to achieve the mission of the organisation, typically by adding competitive advantage and value to its operations. Most of the issues discussed so far do not fall into that category; they were described because they are important areas within the remit of HR where demonstrable benefit can be achieved – for the organisation and for the visibility of your department. However, there is no need to stop at that point. You should now have the audience and the wealth of information needed to play a key role in the strategic process itself.

Strategy is not a question of having a sudden burst of inspiration, but of committed planning and implementation. The key to getting there is the same as for any other form of decision-making, following a logical pattern:

- define the problem to be solved or target to be achieved
- identify the options or alternatives available to you
- establish and gain agreement on key assumptions
- analyse every potentially viable alternative
- obtain any necessary additional information
- check and refine your assumptions and analysis.

It must be remembered that the process of strategic management decision-making always deals with uncertainty. However, changing trends can be noted, such as the increasing customer-driven demand for added value in products and services. Once all the alternatives are listed, the major potential implications of each can be noted. Assessing some of these can be made easier by the use of computer models, but in the final analysis arriving at a decision will require you to make a personal judgement.

Up until now this book has tended to stress two main objectives:

- adding value to the organisation through increasingly effective use of human resources
- managing or assessing the impact of changes imposed by external and internal factors.

Yet to truly add strategic value you will also need to lead the way in capitalising on the competences specific to your organisation. This is not something that you can automate, although good information will be essential. A continuous process of analysis will be required, covering some of the non-HR factors described, in order to understand what is happening to the business and where it is headed.

The intention of this book has been to support the planning process by helping to identify those areas where cost-effective change might be best achieved. It will hopefully be used as an operational tool and act as a constant reference point to ensure that you maintain common standards of quality. At its heart lies the belief that if you can increase the credibility of Personnel, through clear communication with colleagues and visible attainment of financial objectives, then HR will finally gain the strategic recognition it deserves.

To do this will require more than the use of financial frameworks. You will need to identify your internal customers – not just those to whom you are already providing services, but those who may not yet realise what you can offer. For instance, there is an increasing tendency for share-holders to seek short-term returns. However unsatisfactory this is for business life, it is still a potent factor that has to be addressed along with the need for strategies designed to deliver long-term survival for the organisation.

You will also need to ensure that any systems you set up (computer-based or otherwise) are regarded in the department as critical and not mere fripperies. Raising expectations at Board level and then suddenly ceasing to supply them is not a recommended way forward. This means regarding issues like absence and labour turnover in your department as seriously as you regard it elsewhere, which is not always the case.

Don't try to tackle too many areas at once. Not only will your chances of success be reduced on all fronts, but it will be difficult to learn anything useful with an excessive number of variables in operation. Don't target the maximum potential savings in one go. Manage expectations through phased implementation, thereby delivering promised paybacks on schedule.

Finally, you must continuously monitor and report on results being achieved, whether these are good or bad. Only then will your reports be trusted and of value. All new strategies will run into problems: some experiments will fail, forecasts will not always be met, actions may have unanticipated and undesired side effects. Success will only come consistently when all the people involved understand and support the logic of a new strategy. They will then find ways to make it work, rather than compromise or disappear as soon as problems arise. There is a tendency amongst strong-willed individuals, when they want to create change, to try and change actions, but the essence of leadership is to change beliefs first.

Most of this may appear self-evident and also to fall into the 'easier said than done' category. This does not, however, diminish the need to understand properly the objectives of your organisation and to identify those areas in which effective personnel policies can generate a positive contribution. Remember that the mechanistic models are only there as a starting point when you want to quantify these areas. You may need to modify them and will certainly want to refine them over time. Yet they all help to focus on four key targets:

- creating commitment to shared objectives
- establishing credibility
- tracking results
- maintaining credibility.

If you want to take this approach badly enough to overcome the inertia and occasional setbacks that you will encounter, then it will always work to the benefit of you and your organisation. *Credibility* is paramount; it is achieved by doing something in which others can see value.

Another thing to bear in mind is that, for one group of people, controlling HR costs will not really be about improving profitability via individual productivity. It may not even be about understanding and valuing the cost of possible decisions – or the lack of them. For financiers, the control of HR costs is likely to be more about reducing risks, by making the results of those decisions more predictable in financial terms. This poses a potential hazard since, if this approach is allowed to dominate, the organisation may become stultified and lose its competitive edge. It is worth remembering that the whole concept of business risk management is based on *small* but predictable profits. The bigger the profit required, the bigger the risk that will have to be taken. Trying to strike the right balance between timorous caution and compulsive gambling lies at the heart of many a Boardroom disagreement. Too little innovation and your organisation may be killed off; too much and you risk corporate suicide – survival on the middle ground is tricky.

A final hint. When you first make proposals based on this approach, don't raise expectations too high too fast. Halve the potential savings you think you can achieve and set this as your public target. If £200,000 is your target, achieving a saving of £150,000 may be seen as failure; yet if your published target had been £100,000 you would be perceived as having exceeded your plan. Don't, however, underestimate by too much or too often, or people will start loading their interpretation of your next target to compensate.

Recently I gave a talk to a group of experienced HR practitioners and academics. One veteran claimed that there was little new in what I was describing and concluded that 'We've been talking about this approach for more than 30 years.' I believe that the time for talking about it is long gone. Personnel departments are now starting actually to implement similar systems and to gain value from decisions made and monitored through such models. This book should help you make a successful start in your own organisation.

A Glossary of Financial Terms

Use of financial terminology has been deliberately restricted to the bare minimum in this book, since no knowledge or experience of corporate finance could be assumed in the reader. However, in case your appetite has been whetted, this Glossary gives a brief introduction to financial ratios in common use that do *not* make direct use of personnel data.

Unlike HR ratios, most financial ratios can seem fairly abstract; they are certainly less likely to be used as solitary measures. Their great power is that, in combination, they can aid the identification of problems long before these become visible to casual observers – which often includes most of the organisation and its Board, not just outsiders.

Experts will tell you that they can predict which companies are likely to fail or succeed (i.e. not fail) three years before it happens by correct use of these ratios. Indeed, most of the major collapses that hit the headlines have involved claims of manipulation (if not misrepresentation) of one or more of the published ratios. Whether this is true or just self-justification by experts who were bamboozled is hard to disentangle.

Nevertheless, such ratios often lie at the heart of an organisation's credit-rating and thus have a major effect on financing its trading. This, in turn, may impact on the figures from which the ratios are calculated – and so a downward spiral can set in. Using ratios to monitor financial health, therefore, can help avoid failure by reducing risks sufficiently early.

Unlike HR ratios, financial ratios often have intrinsic and recognised values. However, it is still better to use them for comparative exercises – over a number of years (or months), both within the organisation and against competitors. What they do have in common with HR ratios is that there is no correct definition of each one. Variants are often used, but, so long as they are clear and consistently applied, this should not matter.

Example Definitions of Ten Financial Terms Commonly Used in Ratios

Total assets (TA)	= FA + CA + investments, etc
where FA	= fixed assets
and CA	= current assets
Total liabilities (TL)	= CL + EQ + loans, etc
where CL	= current liabilities
and EQ	= equity (issued shares)
Working capital (WC)	= CA − CL.
Retained earnings (RE)	= accumulated reserves = AR.
Debt (DR)	= book value of all SD + LD
where SD	= short-term debt
and LD	= long-term debt.
Market capitalisation (MC)	= SH × SP (if not quoted, book value of equity, reserves and preference)
where SH	= number of issued shares
and SP	= share price.
Capital employed (CE)	= EQ + premium + reserves.
Liquidity (LI)	= number of days (or times) that an organisation could finance its operations from immediate assets if it should cease to generate revenue.
Profitability (PR)	= (PBT × 100)/sales
where PBT	= profit before tax and interest.
Financial risk (FR)	= CL/TA.

Ten Typical Financial Ratios

Current Ratio (CR) = CA/CL
This is the most basic ratio of liquidity and indicates the ability of the organisation to meet debts as they fall due.

Quick Ratio (QR) = [CA − (stock + work-in-progress)]/CL
This is often referred to as the 'acid test' ratio since, unlike CR, it does not include the value of stocks and work-in-progress as part of current assets. It shows whether the organisation has enough cash and near-cash to meet its immediate liabilities.

Profit Margin (PM) = profit/sales
This measures the amount of profit earned on each £ of sales (i.e. the

return on sales) and is often expressed as a percentage, by multiplying PM × 100. Care must be taken to differentiate between gross and net profit margins.

Return on Capital (ROCE) = PBT/CE
A primary ratio of profitability since, unless its ROCE exceeds the cost of its borrowing, an organisation will not survive for long.

Assets Turnover (AT) = sales/FA
A ratio of productivity, with the focus on determining how effectively the assets are being employed.

Interest Cover (IC) = (profit + interest)/interest
This ratio of gearing measures the organisation's ability to service its debts.

Capital Gearing (CG) = DR/EQ
A basic ratio showing the capital leverage of the organisation.

Debtors' Days (DD) = (trade debtors/YTD sales) × number of days YTD
This indicates the organisation's ability to collect outstanding cash, usually calculated every month (or possibly every week). The desired objective is a reduction in DD.

Stock Turn (ST) = costs of sales/stocks
This working capital ratio measures the control of stocks in relation to cost of sales turnover. This is a classic example of where changes in value matter more than any absolute value.

Earnings per Share (EPS) = profit attributable to shareholders/the number of issued equity shares
This is perhaps the most important ratio to a shareholder and a direct measure of growth for an organisation.

There are also other ratios used by those with special interests, such as investors, which may influence their confidence in your organisation even if they say far less about its intrinsic health.

Determining the Degree of Danger

As mentioned, many of these ratios contribute to the financial ratings of an organisation calculated by outside bodies regulatory and commercial. As an example, a brief description is given of *Z-scores*. The concept of Z-scores was devised by Professor Altman in 1968 and many subtle variants now exist. The strength of this approach is that a single score, calculated by the addition of a number of ratios (suitably weighted), has proved a generally reliable predictor of an organisation's security or likelihood of failure – irrespective of the industry type. However, this does not reduce the importance of calculating other ratios for a more rounded picture.

Professor Altman's original Z-score is calculated as follows:

$$Z = (1.2 \times A) + (1.4 \times B) + (3.3 \times C) + (0.6 \times D) + (1.0 \times E)$$

where $A = WC/TA$ $B = RE/TA$
       $C = PBT/TA$ $D = MC/DR$
and $E = sales/TA$.

Professor Altman has said that a Z-score above 3.0 indicates that an organisation should be safe, whilst a Z-score of below 1.8 shows the potential for failure during the next 2-3 years (if not sooner) to be great.

One More Employee-Based Ratio

VAE (or *value added per employee*) is a very basic measure of how effective an organisation is at generating profits from its human resources. SPE (sales per employee), as mentioned in Chapter 1, ignores both the costs of employees and the profitability of revenues achieved. VAE adds a little refinement by this calculation:

$$VAE = (profit + employment\ costs)/employment\ costs.$$

If, for instance, the VAE for your organisation last year was 1.29, then this means that each employee generated an average profit of 29% of their employment costs. This does not, of course, translate into a direct measure of profitability, but it does show the degree of correlation between the costs of employment and profits generated.

A Glossary of HR Terms Used

In each case, the definitions are found in common use in the author's experience. Alternative definitions may be equally suitable, so long as they are applied consistently to all calculations within an organisation.

AB (absenteeism) Any non-scheduled absences (i.e. not holidays or training but including sickness, jury service, etc)

ACR (accession rate) = RH/FTE

ADR (addition rate) = RA/FTE

ATO (acceptances to offers) Number of acceptances received for a particular group of vacancies, divided by the number of offers that had to be issued

BE (benefits) All forms of individual remuneration other than CO (whether or not currently taxed as 'benefits in kind'), such as cars, pensions and loans

BER (benefits expenses ratio) = (BE x 100)/EX

BOR (benefits over revenues) = BE/RE

BPP (benefits per profit) = BE/PR

CO (compensation) All staff cash rewards or incentives, such as salary, wages, overtime, bonuses, commissions – including employee-related taxation (PAYE, NI, etc)

COH (cost of hires) Total of all direct costs for a group of successful hires, divided by the number of people hired

CP (compensation per profit) = (CO + BE)/PR

CR (compensation ratio) = (CO + BE)/EX

EX (expenses) All operating expenditure, excluding tax, interest and extraordinary items

FTE (full-time equivalent) All staff (including part-time and contract) that worked for more than 15 hours per week in that month

HC (headcount) The total FTE at month-end

HRC (human resource costs) = HRE/EX

HRE (human resource expenses) Total operating expenses in the control of the HR department (i.e. remuneration of the team and cost of facilities or equipment used by them, training and staff development budgets, research, IR, communications, etc)

HRH (human resource headcount) Total FTE of the HR department at month-end

HRR (human resource ratio) = HC/HRH

NI (national insurance) Dept of Social Security contributions paid by both employer and employee

PAYE (pay as you earn) Inland Revenue personal income tax deducted under Schedule D

PH (profit per head) = PR/HC

PR (profit) = RE – EX

RA (recruitment additions) RH filling posts new to the organisation

RE (revenues) Total operating income (i.e. total sales) for the period stated

RER (replacement rate) = RF/FTE

RF (recruitment refills) RH filling posts already existing in the organisation

RH (recruitment hires) New employees starting with the organisation

RR (recovery rate) = (CO + BE)/RE

SPE (sales per employee) = RE/HC

TC (training costs) Total costs associated with training during the period, including the expenses of the training department and any direct costs – whoever actually pays for them

TH (training hours) Duration in hours of a course multiplied by the number of attendees at that course, totalled up for all courses over the period

TN (trained numbers) Number of employees who received any training during the period

TTF (time to fill) Total of days taken (from recruitment authorisation to acceptance) for each of a group of vacancies, divided by the number of acceptances

TTH (time to hire) Same as TTF, but taking the longer period from recruitment authorisation to actual start date, again divided by the number of acceptances

UR (utilisation rate) = RE/(CO + BE)

WD (workdays) Average number of days available for work (i.e. excluding authorised absences such as holidays) for the period in question

WR (wage-rate) Average contractual weekly compensation for all employees, excluding overtime

YTD (year to date) Period in days from beginning of current fiscal calendar to date of report.